Methods of Teaching Communication

Methods of Teaching Communication

Deepak Tiwari

CRESCENT
PUBLISHING CORPORATION

[The responsibility for the facts stated, conclusions reached and plagiarism, if any, in this book is entirely that of the Author. And the Publisher bears no responsibility for them, whatsoever.]

Methods of Teaching Communication

Edition : 2026

ISBN 81-8342-020-6

Published by:

CRESCENT PUBLISHING CORPORATION
4806/24, Mathur Lane,
Ansari Road, Darya Ganj,
New Delhi - 110002
Mob.: 9711991838, 9999021668
Ph.No : 011-23244131
e-mail : crescentbook@gmail.com
Website : www.crescentpublishingcorp.weebly.com

Printed at :
Roshan Offset Printers
Delhi

Preface

Communication is the sharing of thoughts, feelings, attitudes, and ideas through the exchange of verbal and nonverbal symbols. We share our private thoughts and feelings with others through communication. The field of communication was founded, in part, because of a felt need to make people better communicators. That meant teaching them how to communicate more effectively, whether it be in public settings or in private. Most of that teaching has happened within the classroom and many professionals have spent their lives instructing others on various aspects of communication.

Teachers are often challenged b teaching communication skills. Their students have already spent most of their lives speaking and listenin an sometimes resist efforts to teach them what they k they already know. Since its introduction as an ac c subject in early twentieth century, very little atte as been paid to the methods involved in teachin unication. Although there have been journal art echniques, and classes on instruction in comm n, there have been few attempts to integrate t sues and concerns that face teachers. The pre e attempts to do that. The activities and strategies described in this book can add some spice into teaching communication skills as well as appeal to different types of learners. It will serve as a highly useful reference tool for teachers, teacher-trainers and students of communication.

Deepak Tiwari

1

Understanding Communication

Communication is the key to learning, for much of what we learn depends on interactions with others. Although all human beings communicate, some individuals, due to the severity of their disabilities, may have limited communication skills. Individuals with severe and multiple disabilities may not have full access to or full control of the multiple means by which most individuals communicate (e.g., speech, facial expressions, body language, print). This inability to express themselves as others would does not mean that these individuals have nothing to say, nor does it diminish their need and right to communicate. Teachers and other service providers must respect this desire to communicate, using their expertise, experience, and commitment to make this possible. As Brown and Gothelf contended, we must assume that individuals with profound disabilities want to control their environment, despite the difficult time they may have doing so.

Some individuals have acquired a few speech skills that enable them to express basic concepts (e.g., requesting a desired food or activity). Limitations in using complex language patterns, however, hamper more abstract communication (e.g., discussing dreams, concerns, future plans). Even though these individuals may have multiple means of communicating without abstract symbols, the ability to clearly express more complex thoughts and feelings is not possible without the use of some kind of system of representative symbols.

Any child who has a disability that interferes with the normal acquisition and development of language will experience difficulties in communicative exchanges (both receptively and expressively). Individuals with severe cognitive disabilities often have difficulty acquiring an abstract means of communication, such as speech or American Sign Language (ASL). Those with autism and severe developmental delays, as well as those with severe sensory impairments (vision or hearing or both), may also find it difficult to communicate effectively.

Certainly a severe physical disability, especially when it is in addition to an intellectual impairment, can hinder the development of speech and language. The intricate physical movements of the oral musculature required for speech are negatively affected by a severe physical disability, and a severe intellectual impairment makes it very difficult for the individual to associate symbols with their referents. According to Haring and Breen, individuals with severe or profound cognitive and physical disabilities may never develop expressive language skills beyond those of a very young child.

What Is Communication ?

Communication occurs when one individual sends a message to another and that message is received and understood. Competence in a symbolic and abstract language system, with formalized rules of word representation, production, and use (e.g., spoken English or

Spanish, manual ASL), is not a prerequisite for communication. In fact, one can be quite facile with a spoken language and not communicate at all if there is no one to talk to, no one present who understands the spoken language used, or no one who is attending to or hearing the message. A trip to a foreign country or an interaction with a preoccupied teenager illustrates this point.

Just as the presence of language does not necessarily mean that communication will follow, the absence of language does not always mean that communication cannot occur. In fact, those not using language can communicate quite well at times. For example, graduate students putting away their papers and pens let the professor know that class has ended; rumbling stomachs and glazed eyes let the principal know that the meeting is over (or should be); and the fidgety behavior of young children who need to·go to the bathroom is easily recognized. For all of these situations and countless others, the absence of symbolic language behavior is irrelevant. In fact, as much as 90% of any message exchanged between two very verbal people can be attributed to nonverbal behavior.

In addition, many nonverbal communicative behaviors are universal. Recognizing the power of nonsymbolic yet highly communicative behavior (e.g., facial expressions, body movements, gestures) is critical for those interested in facilitating the communication skill development of students who are unable to master symbolic languages. Such behaviors form the foundation for enhanced communicative interactions because, unlike speech, they are easier to shape and, therefore, easier to learn.

Kadushin and Kadushin provide a useful general description of the importance of communication:

> Communication is the sharing of thoughts, feelings, attitudes, and ideas through the exchange of verbal and nonverbal symbols. We share our private thoughts and feelings with others through communication. The work derives from communicare, the Latin verb that means to 'make common'.

Pierson and Thomas highlight the importance of communication in social work in detail:

In social work and social welfare agencies, good, clear, accurate communication is essential in several contexts. First, all organizations should provide quality information about services that they offer, which should be widely accessible. This will involve not only a range of languages relevant to their local community but also in electronic, Braille and perhaps taped formats.

Secondly, all workers need to develop appropriate communication skills both for face-to-face and for written communications. The ability to avoid jargon and to communicate in good, clear English and Welsh is of paramount importance. When using other languages, it is equally important that the clear meaning is fully communicated. Workers also need to consider the context in which they are required to speak and to write, and to ensure that they develop a style that is appropriate and relevant for their audience.

Thirdly, some people have specific communication needs. People who take pride in belonging to the deaf community, for example, need to be offered trained competent British Sign Language (BSL) interpreters so that they can communicate clearly in their first language. Some people who have serious communication problems as a result of disability may require specialist support for communication.

Fourthly, agencies that are closely collaborating on projects, working in partnership or negotiating service level agreements need to develop effective channels for communication in order to enhance collaboration.

Fifthly, with the developing emphasis upon a research culture in social welfare, workers need to be able to communicate clearly with funders, research colleagues and research participants in order to produce high quality results and be able to disseminate their findings clearly and imaginatively in order to improve practice.

Finally, communication has a non-verbal dimension. Workers need to be aware of body language, and the importance of listening skills, as part of their effective communication repertoire.

Communication Theory

Communication theory is most commonly associated with systems thinking. Communication relates to the sharing of meaningful interactions with other people in the world. It concerns the passing of, receiving and acting on information.

The theory examines the processes that communication involves: the selection of a means of conveying a message (language, gesture, writing), the decoding of the message by the recipient (hearing, seeing, reading), and making a response on the basis of the interpretation (reply). Understanding the rules and structures of communication can help to formulate sensitive and appropriate professional interactions with the service user.

Interpersonal Communication

One way of defining interpersonal communication is to compare it to other forms of communication. In so doing, we would examine how many people are involved, how physically close they are to one another, how many sensory channels are used, and the feedback provided. Interpersonal communication differs from other forms of communication in that there are few participants involved, the interactants are in close physical proximity to each other, there are many sensory channels used, and feedback is immediate. An important point to note about the contextual definition is that it does not take into account the relationship between the interactants.

We have many different relationships with people. Some researchers say that our definition of interpersonal communication must account for these differences. These researchers say that interacting with a sales clerk in a store is different than the relationship we have with our friends and family members. Thus, some researchers have proposed an alternative way of defining interpersonal communication. This is called the developmental view. From this view, interpersonal communication is defined as communication that occurs between people who have known each other for some time. Importantly, these people view each other as unique individuals, not as people who are simply acting out social situations.

Functions

Interpersonal communication is important because of the functions its achieves. Whenever we engage in communication with another person, we seek to gain information about them. We also give off information through a wide variety of verbal and nonverbal cues. Read more about the various functions of interpersonal communication and then complete the interactive activity and the quiz at the end of this unit.

Gaining Information

One reason we engage in interpersonal communication is so that we can gain knowledge about another individual. Social Penetration Theory says that we attempt to gain information about others so that we can interact with them more effectively. We can better predict how they will think, feel, and act if we know who they are. We gain this information passively, by observing them; actively, by having others engage them; or interactively, by engaging them ourselves. Self-disclosure is often used to get information from another person.

Building a Context of Understanding

We also engage in interpersonal communication to help us better understand what someone says in a given context. The words we say can mean very different things depending on how they are said or in what context.

Meaning Assigned to Communication

— *Content Messages* refer to the surface level meaning of a message.

— *Relationship Messages* refer to how a message is said. The two are sent simultaneously, but each affects the meaning assigned to the communication. Interpersonal communication helps us understand each other better.

Establishing Identity

Another reason we engage in interpersonal communication is to establish an identity. The roles we play in our relationships help us establish identity. So too does the face, the public self-image we present to others. Both roles and face are constructed based on how we interact with others.

Interpersonal Needs

Finally, we engage in interpersonal communication because we need to express and receive interpersonal needs. William Schutz has identified three such needs: inclusion, control, and affection.

- Inclusion is the need to establish identity with others.
- Control is the need to exercise leadership and prove one's abilities. Groups provide outlets for this need. Some individuals do not want to be a leader. For them, groups provide the necessary control over aspects of their lives.
- Affection is the need to develop relationships with people. Groups are an excellent way to make friends and establish relationships

Relationship Development

Researchers have studied relationships to understand how they develop. One of the most popular models for understanding relationship development is Mark Knapp's Relational Stages Model. Knapp's model works well to describe many types of relationships: romantic couples, friends, busines partners, roommates, etc. Other models have also been discussed. For instance, Stephen Duck's Relationship Filtering Model is another way of looking at how relationships begin. Read about these models and then complete an interactive activity and short quiz to test your knowledge.

Knapp's Relationship Escalation Model:

— *Initiation:* This stage is very short, sometimes as short as 10-15 seconds. In this stage, interactants are concerned with making favorable impressions on each other. They may use standard greetings or observe each other's appearance or mannerisms.

— *Experimenting:* In the next stage, individuals ask questions of each other in order to gain information about them and decide if they wish to continue the relationship. "Many relationships progress no further than this point".

— *Intensifying*: Self-disclosure becomes more common in the intensifying stage. The relationship becomes less formal, the interactants begin to see each other as individuals, and statements are made about the level of commitment each has to thc relationship.

— *Integrating*: The individuals become a pair in the integrating stage. They begin to do things together and, importantly, others come to see them as a pair. A shared relational identity starts to form in this stage.

— *Bonding:* During the bonding stage, a formal, sometimes legal, announcement of the relationship is made. Examples include a marriage, "best friend" ritual, or business partnership agreement. Few relationships reach this level.

Duck's Relationship Filtering Model:

— *Sociological/Incidental Cues*: Duck's model is a set of filters through which we make choices about the level of relationship we wish to pursue with others. The first filter, socioligical/incidental cues, describes the constraints placed on our meeting people due to where we live or work. In other words, given our sociological location, there are some people we see a lot of and others we never meet.

— *Preinteraction Cues*: Information we gain about people before we even interact with them leads us to exclude or include individuals with whom we wish to have a relationship. For instance, the appearance of some individuals will cause you to avoid or approach them.

— *Interaction Cues*: As we begin to interact with others, we make judgments about whether to include or exclude them from possible relationships.

— *Cognitive Cues*: At the deepest level, we make judgments about people based on their personality and the degree to which we think it will match ours. As others reach this level, we consider them "best friends."

Knapp's Relationship Termination Model:

— *Differentiating* : In this stage, partners begin to stress the "me" instead of the "we." In other words, the individuals begin to assert their independence. They may develop different hobbies or activities. The relationship may continue to dissolve, or this stage may be a warning sign that the couple needs to address their relationship status.

— *Circumscribing*: Communication between the couple diminishes during this stage. They tend to avoid certain topics of discussion. Outwardly, the couple appears normal. At this stage, attempts can be made to discuss the relationship and return it to a positive state.

— *Stagnating*: During the stagnating stage, the individuals avoid discussing the relationship because they think they know what the other will say. Others begin to take notice that something is wrong.

— *Avoiding*: The pair begins to physically separate themselves during the avoiding stage. The individuals try to reduce the opportunities for discussion.

— *Terminating:* This is the final stage of the relationship. Termination may come naturally, such as at the end of the semester when roommates move out, or arbitrarily, through divorce. Termination of the relationship can occur positively or negatively.

Self-Disclosure

Self-disclosure is seen as a useful strategy for sharing information with others. By sharing information, we become more intimate with other people and our interpersonal relationship is strengthened. Read about self-disclosure and then complete the interactive activity and take a short quiz to test your understanding of the concept. Self-disclosure is not simply providing information to another person. Instead, scholars define self-disclosure as sharing information with others that they would not normally know or discover. Self-disclosure involves risk and vulnerability on the part of the person sharing the information.

The Johari Window

A useful way of viewing self-disclosure is the Johari window. The Johari window is a way of showing how much information you know about yourself and how much others know about you. The window contains four panes, as shown below.

	Known to self	Unknown to self
Known to others	Open self	Blind self
Not known to others	Known self	Unknown self

The Open Self includes information such as hair color, occupation, and physical appearance. The Blind Self includes information that others can see in you, but you cannot see in your self. You might think you are poor leader, but others think you exhibit strong leadership skills. The Known Self contains information you wish to keep private, such as dreams or ambitions. The Unknown Self includes everything that you and others do not know about yourself. You may have hidden talents, for example, that you have not explored. Through self-disclosure, we open and close panes so that we may become more intimate with others.

Functions of Self-Disclosure

Self-disclosure performs several functions. It is a way of gaining information about another person. We want to be able to predict the thoughts and actions of people we know. Self-disclosure is one way to learn about how another person thinks and feels. Once one person engages in self-disclosure, it is implied that the other person will also disclose personal information. This is known as the norm of reciprocity. Mutual disclosure deepens trust in the relationships and helps both people understand each other more. You also come to feel better about yourself and your relationship when the other person accepts what you tell them.

Risks of Self-Disclosure

While there are several advantages to self-disclosure, there are also risks. One risk is that the person will not respond favorably to the information. Self-disclosure does not automatically lead to favorable impressions. Another risk is that the other person will gain power in the relationship because of the information they possess. Finally, too much self-disclosure or self-disclosure that comes too early in a relationship can damage the relationship. Thus, while self-disclosure is useful, it can also be damaging to a relationship.

Relational Patterns

As relationships progress, patterns of interactions take shape that we may not recognize. This section describes some of these patterns. Complete the interactive activity at the end of the unit and then take a quiz to test your knowledge.

Rigid Role Relations

There are two basic types of behaviors in relationships: dominance and submissiveness. Dominance is often referred to as one-up, while submissiveness, one-down. In some relationships, the two are complementary—one individual is one-up, the other one-down—and the relationship is rewarding. Other relationships are symmetrical, where both parties are one-up or both are one-down. Problems can result when individuals feel trapped by their role as the dominant or submissive member of the relationship. Flexibility can help both partners enjoy the relationship.

Disconfirmations

Whenever we communicate with someone else, we open ourselves up for rejection. The other individual can accept what we say or reject what we say. Researcher Evelyn Sieburg has identified seven "disconfirming" responses that reject the other individual.

— *Impervious*: Failing to acknowledge the other person.

— *Interrupting*: Cutting the other's message short.

— *Irrelevant*: Giving a response that is unrelated to what the other has said.

— *Tangential*: Briefly responding to the other's message.

— *Impersonal*: Responding by using formal, jargon-laden language.

— *Incoherent*: Responding with a rambling, difficult to understand message.

— *Incongruous*: Giving contradictory verbal and nonverbal messages.

Spirals

A third type of relational pattern is a spiral. "In a spiral, one partner's behavior intensifies that of the other". Spirals can be progressive, in which one partner's behavior leads to increasing levels of satisfaction for the other. Spirals can also be regressive, where one partner's communication leads to increasing dissatisfaction. Stopping regressive spirals from getting out of control depends on the open communication between the two individuals.

Dependencies and Counterdependencies

A final type of relational pattern is dependencies and counterdependencies. In a dependency relationship, one individual sees himself or herself relying on another person for something. Soon, he or she agrees with whatever the other says or does. In a counterdependency, one individual sees himself or herself as not being dependent on the other. Thus, he or she disagrees with the other quite frequently

Interpersonal Conflict

Conflict is a part of most every interpersonal relationship. Managing conflict, then, is important if the relationship is to be long-lasting and rewarding. Learn how to manage conflict in your relationships and then complete the activity.

Conflict has been defined as "an expressed struggle between at least two interdependent parties who perceive incompatible goals, scarce resources, and interference from the other party in achieving their goals". Important concepts in this definition include "expressed struggle," which means the two sides must communicate about the problem for there to be conflict. Another important idea is that conflict often involves perceptions. The two sides may only perceive that their goals, resources, and interference is incompatible with each other's.

Common Problems in Conflict Management

Researchers have identified several problems that typically arise in conflict situations. First, the parties will simply avoid the conflict. This can be damaging, because it can lead to greater problems in the future. It is usually best that the individuals discuss their differences. Second, individuals involved in conflict may blame the other individual. Often, individuals go beyond the specific behavior in question and blame the character of the person. When people use words such as, "He's such a slob," they are engaging in blame the other behavior. A final problem that is often encountered in conflict management is adopting a win-lose mentality. Focusing on each individual's goals/outcomes will help avoid using a win-lose strategy.

Defensive climate

The climate in which conflict is managed is important. Dyads should avoid a defensive climate, which is characterized by these qualities:

— *Evaluation*: judging and criticizing other group members.

— *Control*: imposing the will of one group member on the others.

— *Strategy*: using hidden agendas.

— *Neutrality*: demonstrating indifference and lack of commitment.

— *Superiority*: expressing dominance.

— *Certainty*: being rigid in one's willingness to listen to others.

Supportive Climate

Instead, individuals should foster a supportive climate, marked by these traits:

— *Description*: presenting ideas or opinions.

- *Problem orientation*: focusing attention on the task.
- *Spontaneity*: communicating openly and honestly.
- *Empathy*: understanding another person's thoughts.
- *Equality*: asking for opinions.
- *Provisionalism*: expressing a willingness to listen other the ideas of others.

Additional Tips

A few final tips can help insure that conflict is successfully managed:

- *Conflict Can Be Constructive*: Recognize that conflict can strengthen your relationships.
- *Be Prepared*. Plan how you will communicate about conflict in order to create a supportive climate.
- *Be Involved*. Do not withdraw from the conflict or avoid conflict situations.
- *Withhold Quick Retorts*. Be careful about what you say and how you say it.
- *Review*. Summarize what you have discussed and make plans to continue the discussion if time permits immediate resolution.

Non-verbal Communication

Non-verbal communication can be broadly divided into two area: proxemics concerned with distance and how close people like to be to each other and kinesics referring to movements, gestures, expression and eye contact. More simply we can consider the following areas: distance, posture and orientation, gaze and eye contact, and facial expression. For Kadushin and Kadushin, non-verbal communication includes:

1. chronomics (time keeping)
2. artifactual communication (personal attire/dress)
3. smell (body odours)
4. touch (handshaking, hugs)
5. paralinguistic (how words are said in terms of their tone, pitch, volume, speed, emphasis, intonation, articulation and intensity)
6. proxemics (space and distance)
7. body language-kinesics (movement, gesture and body posture particularly in relation to the eyes, face, hands, legs and feet).

Body Language

Detailed studies have identified many items in the nonverbal vocabulary, including five thousand distinctly different hand gestures have been identified and one thousand different steady body postures. Precise observation of nonverbal behaviour is important, but it is only a first step. The interviewer still has to infer some valid meaning from the data. Accurate observation is necessary but insufficient for understanding the psychological relevance of the gesture.

Needs of Communication Intervention

When students demonstrate such minimal communication skills that they are not adequately expressing themselves, others tend to assume that they have nothing to communicate or simply do not care about anything. Unfortunately, such assumptions are dangerous because they dehumanize the student, casting him or her in an extremely dependent and vulnerable position. Following the least dangerous assumption, it is always preferable to perceive all students, regardless of the severity of the disability, as individuals who have something to say but who have extreme difficulty making their thoughts heard and understood by others. With this latter assumption, it is the responsibility of those who communicate with greater ease to do whatever they can to help the student understand what is being said and to find a way to give him or her a "voice."

Operating on the assumption that all individuals need to communicate, the tendency to wait until certain "prerequisite skills" are demonstrated before providing helpful intervention makes little sense. Mirenda firmly stated that breathing is the only real prerequisite to communication. The process to determine whether students with severe disabilities qualify for communication intervention becomes extremely simple given such a prerequisite. The question, then, should be not whether students with severe disabilities will benefit from communication intervention but how best to provide that support.

Unfortunately, practitioners in many states seem to be spending valuable time and energy determining eligibility for communication intervention services. Several parents and teachers have expressed to the author their frustration at not being able to gain access to quality speech-language therapy services for a student who does not speak. When speech becomes a prerequisite for communication intervention, many students with severe disabilities will be denied important support. Several states adhere to a model of cognitive referencing to determine eligibility for intervention services.

Cognitive referencing is the practice of identifying a discrepancy between a child's cognitive and language abilities to qualify for services. For children with severe intellectual challenges who are determined to have similar speech-language and cognitive abilities, communication services can be considered irrelevant. Presumably these children would not benefit from intervention. However common this approach may be, the belief that children with equal delays in both language and cognitive development are not able to benefit from language intervention has not been substantiated. These children can and do benefit. If anything, the assessment procedures used to determine eligibility are questionable.

2

Teaching Communication Skills

We all can use effective communication skills, and giving our children a head start in this arena is one of the many kindnesses, not to mention neccessities we need to arm our children with. One of the hallmarks of a well-socialized child is the child's ability to effectively communicate with people their own age as well as people older than they. The ability to effectively communicate helps boost a child's confidence immensely. It is as important as being able to do long division, or to spell well, or to read.

One of the more effective tools for learning how to speak effectively is by simply having dinner around the table every night, with the children being encouraged to speak, with no one putting them down for their opinions. It is in this environment that children learn to speak as well as to listen, with love.

When the boys were small, we would tell them a story, such as a story about a dog. We would give one of the boys a bell, and every time we read the word "dog" they were to ring the bell. This is a highly effective means of getting them to listen, and it is one of the oldest games in the book. We taught them how to take a phone message, and how to dial 911 or Grandma's, whichever they thought was most effective in their particular emergency.

In teaching our children effective speaking to others, it is important to encourage them to ask questions of strangers, (within reason, of course) and to speak to strangers. Until they are older, they need you right there to help them out, and for protection. It is important that they know how to start and sustain a conversation, look someone in the eye while speaking and listening, how to speak in a tone that is loud enough while not being offensive, and how to cut off a conversation. Good manners and good language usage become more important when you get to actually use them! Ineffective communication skills are supposed to be one of the major reasons why couples divorce, so in this world, good communication is not only enlightening, it is also a tool for survival!

Cultural Importance of Teaching Communication

Communication is an essential skill utilized by any teacher. It is important to be a culturally competent communicator. It is also important to identify the belief systems of both the student and teacher to spot blocks to communication:

— *Ethnocentralism*: Inability to accept anothers culture's world view; "my way is the best"

— *Discrimination*:Differential treatment of an individual due to minority status; actual and perceived; e.g., "we just aren't equipped to serve people like that."

— *Stereotyping*: Generalizing about a person while ignoring presence of individual difference; e.g., "she's like that because she's Asian — all Asians are nonverbal."

— *Cultural Blindness*: Differences are ignored and one proceeds as though differences did not exist; e.g., "there's no need to worry about a person's culture — if you're a sensitive teacher, you do okay."

— *Cultural Impossition*: Belief that everyone should conform to the majority; e.g., "we know what's best for you, if you don't like it you can go elsewhere."

Concepts related to bridging cultural differences include:

E — Everyone has a culture.

T — Take time to collect relevant cultural information.

H —Hold all judgements; ie. be careful about interpreting the culturally different student's behavior, especially if unfamiliar with the culture.

N —Notice and negotiate differences in understanding of teaching and learning.

I — Involve cultural resources as approtriate.

C —Collaborate to develop objectives and educational strategies

Activities Teaching Communication

Teachers are often challenged by teaching communication skills. Their students have already spent most of their lives speaking and listening and sometimes resist efforts to teach them what they think they already know. The following activities can add some spice into teaching communication skills as well as appeal to different types of learners.

Jigsaw Puzzle Method

— Divide students into three groups. Tell the groups that they all have a common goalXto put together a jigsaw puzzle in a limited amount of time. However, each group speaks a different language from the other groups. Each groups language consists of only one word. Assign each group a nonsense word. For example, you might assign group one the word cariffle, group two woobidee, and group three varipipip.

— Divide the pieces of a jigsaw puzzle among the three groups. Tell groups they have two minutes to plan how they want to communicate with the other groups to put together the puzzle. During this planning phase, group members may communicate freely with one another. When the groups join together to build the puzzle, the only words that may be spoken are the nonsense words assigned to each group. For example, group one may only say cariffle while members of group two may only say woobidee. Students must rely on varying the variety, quality, rate, and volume of their vocal communication in order to accomplish their goal.

— Give groups five minutes to try to put the puzzle together. Remind them to only use their assigned word and to try to communicate by varying their vocal characteristics. Ask students to share their insights on what happened during the activity. Discuss how students were able to communicate vocally, even when the words they used were nonsense.

I See What You are Saying

— Divide students into groups of three. Near each group, place two chairs back to back. Ask two students to sit in the chairs. Tell the third student to face one of the sitting students. Ask the sitting student facing the standing student to describe a funny situation he or she has experienced. The person sitting with his or her back to the speaker should listen closely. The person facing the storyteller should carefully observe the speakers facial expressions, gestures, and other nonverbal movements.

-- Tell the person who sat with his or her back to the speaker to report to his or her group what the story was. Tell groups to compare perceptions of the student who watched the speaker and the participant who only listened. Discuss the following questions with the entire group:

  - Did the observers tend to see and hear the same message as the listener? Why or why not?
  - How did the speakers feel knowing that their words and actions were being closely monitored? In real-life situations, how do you handle feelings of being watched by others as you speak?
  - How does nonverbal communication affect communication with employees with disabilities such as visual impairments or hearing impairments?

Whats In It For Me?

Before the class session, choose a short article from a newspaper, magazine, or journal to share with the class. The subject isnt important, but the article should have a lot of details in it. Casually mention at the beginning of a class period that you read an interesting article and would like to share it with them. Read the article to the class. After youve finished reading the article, pull out a one dollar bill and say, Okay, Ive got a few questions for you based on the article you just heard. Whoever gets all the questions right wins this dollar. Have each student take out a blank sheet of paper.

Ask students eight to ten questions based on details from the article. Ask them to write their answers on the sheet of paper. Have students switch papers and then tell them the answers. Ask if anyone knew the answers to all of the questions. It is unlikely that any one person will have answered all of the questions correctly. Give the dollar bill to the student with the most correct answers. Say to students, You all heard the story, yet few of you could remember very much about it. Ask students why they didnt remember much after listening to the story. Discuss how they could improve their listening skills and whether they would have listened more attentively if they had known ahead of time that there would be a prize. Discuss how the four stages of active listening could have helped them.

Game Shows

— Divide students into three teams. Ask Team A to prepare a six-question short-answer quiz on vocal communication. Allow five minutes. Ask Teams B and C to review their class notes on the topic while Team A prepares its quiz. Tell Team A to ask Team B one of its questions. If Team B cannot answer the question or answers incorrectly, Team C may try to answer the question. Team A directs its next question to Team C first and repeats the process. Team A continues to ask questions until the quiz is done.

— Ask Team B to prepare a similar quiz on verbal communication. Ask Teams A and C to review their class notes on verbal communication while Team B prepares its quiz. Repeat the quiz process from above. Ask Team C to prepare a similar quiz on listening skills while Teams A and B review their class notes. Repeat the quiz process again.

Listening in Motion

— Divide students into pairs. Ask partners to take turns explaining a concept learned in one of their other classes. For example, they might explain how to write a geometry proof, or what a feudalistic governmental system is, or the theme of a book they read in literature. Remind the listening partner in each pair to use the active listening techniques you have taught (such as mirroring, paraphrasing, summarizing, self-disclosure, and clarifying questions). Spend a minute or two with each pair to make sure they are using active listening skills correctly. Offer praise or suggestions for improvement when necessary. Ask each pair to demonstrate to another pair their effective use of active listening skills.

Listen to What I Hear

— Ask two volunteers to give you directions to their homes. Practice good listening techniques with the first person and poor listening techniques with the second. Ask students what you did that showed you were a good listener in the first example and what you did that showed you were a poor listener in the second.

Improving Non-verbal Communication Skills

It is not only what you say in the classroom that is important, but it's how you say it that can make the difference to students. Nonverbal messages are an essential component of communication in the teaching process.

Teachers should be aware of nonverbal behavior in the classroom for three major reasons:

— An awareness of nonverbal behavior will allow you to become better receivers of students' messages.

— You will become a better sender of signals that reinforce learning.

— This mode of communication increases the degree of the perceived psychological closeness between teacher and student.

Major Areas of Nonverbal Behaviors

Some major areas of nonverbal behaviors to explore are:

— Eye contact

— Facial expressions

— Gestures

— Posture and body orientation

— Proximity

— Paralinguistics

— Humor

Eye contact

Eye contact, an important channel of interpersonal communication, helps regulate the flow of communication. And it signals interest in others. Furthermore, eye contact with audiences increases the speaker's credibility. Teachers who make eye contact open the flow of communication and convey interest, concern, warmth and credibility.

Facial expressions

Smiling is a powerful cue that transmits:

— Happiness

— Friendliness

— Warmth

— Liking

— Affiliation

Thus, if you smile frequently you will be perceived as more likable, friendly, warm and approachable. Smiling is often contagious and students will react favorably and learn more.

Gestures

If you fail to gesture while speaking, you may be perceived as boring, stiff and unanimated. A lively and animated teaching style captures students' attention, makes the material more interesting, facilitates learning and provides a bit of entertainment. Head nods, a form of gestures, communicate positive reinforcement to students and indicate that you are listening.

Very few gestures are universally understood and interpreted. What is perfectly acceptable may be rude, or even obscene, in other cultures.

It is important for mainstream teachers to understand how the gestures they use unconsciously may be misunderstood. This activity allows participants to look a little closer at how body language might be interpreted by learners and their parents.

Demonstrate the gestures below and ask participants to write down what they think each gesture means. Participants should also indicate if they think the gesture is considered rude in the United States. Have group discuss how body language could influence communication between cultures.

— Beckon with index finger.

— Point at something in the room using index finger.

— Make a "V" sign.

— Smile.

— Sit with sole of feet or shoe showing.

— Form a circle with fingers to indicate "O.K."

— Pat a student on the head.

— Pass an item to someone with one hand.

— Wave hand with palm facing outward to greet someone.

— Nod head up and down to say "Yes."

Each of the following responses give a general guide to cultural differences in the meaning of gestures.

1. *Beckon with index finger*. This means "Come here" in the U.S. To motion with the index finger to call someone is insulting, or even obscene, in many cultures. Expect a reaction when you beckon to a student from the Middle or Far East; Portugal, Spain, Latin America, Japan, Indonesia and Hong Kong. It is more acceptable to beckon with the palm down, with fingers or whole hand waving.

2. *Point at something in the room using index finger*. It is impolite to point with the index finger in the Middle

and Far East. Use an open hand or your thumb (in Indonesia)

3. *Make a "V" sign.* This means "Victory" in most of Europe when you make this sign with your palm facing away from you. If you face your palm in, the same gesture means "Shove it."

4. *Smile.* This gesture is universally understood. However, it various cultures there are different reasons for smiling. The Japanese may smile when they are confused or angry. In other parts of Asia, people may smile when they are embarrassed. People in other cultures may not smile at everyone to indicate a friendly greeting as we do in the United States. A smile may be reserved for friends. It is important not to judge students or their parents because they do not smile, or smile at what we would consider "inappropriate" times.

5. *Sit with soles shoes showing.* In many cultures this sends a rude message. In Thailand, Japan and France as well as countries of the Middle and Near East showing the soles of the feet demonstrates disrespect. You are exposing the lowest and dirtiest part of your body so this is insulting.

6. *Form a circle with fingers to indicate "O.K."* Although this means "O.K." in the U.S. and in many countries around the world, there are some notable exceptions:

   — In Brazil and Germany, this gesture is obscene.

   — In Japan, this means "money."

   — In France, it has the additional meaning of "zero" or "worthless."

7. *Pat a student on the head.* This is very upsetting to students from Asia. The head is the repository of the soul in the Buddhist religion. Children from cultures which are influenced by Buddhism will feel uncomfortable if their head is touched.

8. *Pass an item to someone with one hand.* In Japan this is very rude. Even a very small item such as a pencil must be passed with two hands. In many Middle and Far Eastern countries it is rude to pass something with your left hand which is considered "unclean."

9. *Wave hand with the palm facing outward to greet someone.* In Europe, waving the hand back and forth can mean "No." To wave "good-bye," raise the palm outward and wag the fingers in unison, This is also a serious insult in Nigeria if the hand is too close to another person's face.

10. *Nod head up and down to say "Yes."* In Bulgaria and Greece, this gesture means "No."

Posture and body orientation

You communicate numerous messages by the way you walk, talk, stand and sit. Standing erect, but not rigid, and leaning slightly forward communicates to students that you are approachable, receptive and friendly. Furthermore, interpersonal closeness results when you and your students face each other. Speaking with your back turned or looking at the floor or ceiling should be avoided; it communicates disinterest to your class.

Proximity

Cultural norms dictate a comfortable distance for interaction with students. You should look for signals of discomfort caused by invading students' space. Some of these are:

— Rocking

— Leg swinging

— Tapping

— Gaze aversion

Typically, in large college classes space invasion is not a problem. In fact, there is usually too much distance. To counteract this, move around the classroom to increase interaction with your students. Increasing proximity enables you to make better eye contact and increases the opportunities for students to speak.

Paralinguistics

This facet of nonverbal communication includes such vocal elements as:

— Tone

— Pitch

— Rhythm

— Timbre

— Loudness

— Inflection

For maximum teaching effectiveness, learn to vary these six elements of your voice. One of the major criticisms is of instructors who speak in a monotone. Listeners perceive these instructors as boring and dull. Students report that they learn less and lose interest more quickly when listening to teachers who have not learned to modulate their voices.

Humor

Humor is often overlooked as a teaching tool, and it is too often not encouraged in college classrooms. Laughter releases stress and tension for both instructor and student. You should develop the ability to laugh at yourself and encourage students to do the same. It fosters a friendly classroom environment that facilitates learning.

Obviously, adequate knowledge of the subject matter is crucial to your success; however, it's not the only crucial element. Creating a climate that facilitates learning and retention demands good nonverbal and verbal skills. To improve your nonverbal skills, record your speaking on video tape. Then ask a colleague in communications to suggest refinements.

3

Teaching Listening

Instructors want to produce students who, even if they do not have complete control of the grammar or an extensive lexicon, can fend for themselves in communication situations. In the case of listening, this means producing students who can use listening strategies to maximize their comprehension of aural input, identify relevant and non-relevant information, and tolerate less than word-by-word comprehension.

The Process of Listening

To accomplish this goal, instructors focus on the process of listening rather than on its product.

— They develop students' awareness of the listening process and listening strategies by asking students to think and talk about how they listen in their native language.

— They allow students to practice the full repertoire of listening strategies by using authentic listening tasks.

— They behave as authentic listeners by responding to student communication as a listener rather than as a teacher.

— When working with listening tasks in class, they show students the strategies that will work best for the listening purpose and the type of text. They explain how and why students should use the strategies.

— They have students practice listening strategies in class and ask them to practice outside of class in their listening assignments. They encourage students to be conscious of what they're doing while they complete listening tape assignments.

— They encourage students to evaluate their comprehension and their strategy use immediately after completing an assignment. They build comprehension checks into in-class and out-of-class listening assignments, and periodically review how and when to use particular strategies.

— They encourage the development of listening skills and the use of listening strategies by using the target language to conduct classroom business: making announcements, assigning homework, describing the content and format of tests.

— They do not assume that students will transfer strategy use from one task to another. They explicitly mention how a particular strategy can be used in a different type of listening task or with another skill.

By raising students' awareness of listening as a skill that requires active engagement, and by explicitly teaching listening strategies, instructors help their students develop both the ability and the confidence to handle communication situations they may encounter beyond the classroom. In this way they give their students the foundation for communicative competence in the new language.

Challenges of Teaching Listening Skills

Teaching listening skills is one of the most difficult tasks for any teacher. This is because successful listening skills are acquired over time and with lots of practice. It's frustrating for students because there are no rules as in grammar teaching. Speaking and writing also have very specific exercises that can lead to improved skills. This is not to say that there are not ways of improving listening skills, however they are difficult to quantify.

One of the largest inhibitors for students is often mental block. While listening, a student suddenly decides that he or she doesn't understand what is being said. At this point, many students just tune out or get caught up in an internal dialogue trying translate a specific word. Some students convince themselves that they are not able to understand well and create problems for themselves.

They key to helping students improve their listening skills is to convince them that not understanding is OK. This is more of an attitude adjustment than anything else, and it is easier for some students to accept than others. Another important point the teachers try to teach the students (with differing amounts of success) is that they need to listen as often as possible, but for short periods of time.

Many teachers like to use this analogy: Imagine you want to get in shape. You decide to begin jogging. The very first day you go out and jog seven miles. If you are lucky, you might even be able to jog the seven miles. However, chances are good that you will not soon go out jogging again. Fitness trainers have taught us that we must begin with little steps. Begin jogging short distances and walk some as well, over time you can build up the distance. Using this approach, you'll be much more likely to continue jogging and get fit.

Students need to apply the same approach to listening skills. Encourage them to get a film, or listen to an English radio station, but not to watch an entire film or listen for two hours. Students should often listen, but they should listen for short periods - five to ten minutes. This should happen four or five times a week. Even if they don't understand anything, five to ten minutes is a minor investement. However, for this strategy to work, students must not expect improved understanding too quickly. The brain is capable of amazing things if given time, students must have the patience to wait for results. If a student continues this exercise over two to three months their listening comprehension skills will greatly improve.

Integrating Metacognitive Strategies

Before listening: Plan for the listening task

— Set a purpose or decide in advance what to listen for

— Decide if more linguistic or background knowledge is needed

— Determine whether to enter the text from the top down (attend to the overall meaning) or from the bottom up (focus on the words and phrases)

During and after listening: Monitor comprehension

— Verify predictions and check for inaccurate guesses

— Decide what is and is not important to understand

— Listen/view again to check comprehension

— Ask for help

After listening: Evaluate comprehension and strategy use

— Evaluate comprehension in a particular task or area

— Evaluate overall progress in listening and in particular types of listening tasks

— Decide if the strategies used were appropriate for the purpose and for the task

— Modify strategies if necessary

Using Authentic Materials and Situations

Authentic materials and situations prepare students for the types of listening they will need to do when using the language outside the classroom.

One-Way Communication

Materials:

— Radio and television programs

— Public address announcements (airports, train/bus stations, stores)

— Speeches and lectures

— Telephone customer service recordings

Procedure:

— Help students identify the listening goal: to obtain specific information; to decide whether to continue listening; to understand most or all of the message

— Help students outline predictable sequences in which information may be presented: who-what-when-where (news stories); who-flight number-arriving/departing-gate number (airport announcements); "for [function], press [number]" (telephone recordings)

— Help students identify key words/phrases to listen for

Two-Way Communication

In authentic two-way communication, the listener focuses on the speaker's meaning rather than the speaker's language. The focus shifts to language only when meaning is not clear. Note the difference between the teacher as teacher and the teacher as authentic listener in the dialogues in the popup screens.

Strategies for Developing Listening Skills

Language learning depends on listening. Listening provides the aural input that serves as the basis for language acquisition and enables learners to interact in spoken communication.

Effective language instructors show students how they can adjust their listening behavior to deal with a variety of situations, types of input, and listening purposes. They help students develop a set of listening strategies and match appropriate strategies to each listening situation.

Listening Strategies

Listening strategies are techniques or activities that contribute directly to the comprehension and recall of listening input. Listening strategies can be classified by how the listener processes the input.

Top-down strategies are listener based; the listener taps into background knowledge of the topic, the situation or context, the type of text, and the language. This background knowledge activates a set of expectations that help the listener to interpret what is heard and anticipate what will come next. Top-down strategies include

— listening for the main idea

— predicting

— drawing inferences

— summarizing

Bottom-up strategies are text based; the listener relies on the language in the message, that is, the combination of sounds, words, and grammar that creates meaning. Bottom-up strategies include

— listening for specific details

— recognizing cognates

— recognizing word-order patterns

Strategic listeners also use *metacognitive strategies* to plan, monitor, and evaluate their listening.

— They plan by deciding which listening strategies will serve best in a particular situation.

— They monitor their comprehension and the effectiveness of the selected strategies.

— They evaluate by determining whether they have achieved their listening comprehension goals and whether the combination of listening strategies selected was an effective one.

Listening for Meaning

To extract meaning from a listening text, students need to follow four basic steps:

— Figure out the purpose for listening. Activate background knowledge of the topic in order to predict or anticipate content and identify appropriate listening strategies.

— Attend to the parts of the listening input that are relevant to the identified purpose and ignore the rest. This selectivity enables students to focus on specific items in the input and reduces the amount of information they have to hold in short-term memory in order to recognize it.

— Select top-down and bottom-up strategies that are appropriate to the listening task and use them flexibly and interactively. Students' comprehension improves and their confidence increases when they use top-down and bottom-up strategies simultaneously to construct meaning.

— Check comprehension while listening and when the listening task is over. Monitoring comprehension helps students detect inconsistencies and comprehension failures, directing them to use alternate strategies.

Developing Listening Activities

As you design listening tasks, keep in mind that complete recall of all the information in an aural text is an unrealistic expectation to which even native speakers are not usually held. Listening exercises that are meant to train should be success-oriented and build up students' confidence in their listening ability.

Construct the listening activity around a contextualized task.

Contextualized listening activities approximate real-life tasks and give the listener an idea of the type of information to expect and what to do with it in advance of the actual listening. A beginning level task would be locating places on a map (one way) or exchanging name and address information (two way). At an intermediate level students could follow directions for assembling something (one way) or work in pairs to create a story to tell to the rest of the class (two way).

Define the activity's instructional goal and type of response.

Each activity should have as its goal the improvement of one or more specific listening skills. A listening activity may have more than one goal or outcome, but be careful not to overburden the attention of beginning or intermediate listeners.

Recognizing the goal(s) of listening comprehension in each listening situation will help students select appropriate listening strategies.

— *Identification*: Recognizing or discriminating specific aspects of the message, such as sounds, categories of words, morphological distinctions

— *Orientation*: Determining the major facts about a message, such as topic, text type, setting

— *Main idea comprehension*: Identifying the higher-order ideas

— *Detail comprehension*: Identifying supporting details

— *Replication*: Reproducing the message orally or in writing

Check the level of difficulty of the listening text.

The factors listed below can help you judge the relative ease or difficulty of a listening text for a particular purpose and a particular group of students.

— *How is the information organized?* Does the story line, narrative, or instruction conform to familiar expectations? Texts in which the events are presented in natural chronological order, which have an informative title, and which present the information following an obvious organization (main ideas first, details and examples second) are easier to follow.

— *How familiar are the students with the topic?* Remember that misapplication of background knowledge due to cultural differences can create major comprehension difficulties.

— *Does the text contain redundancy?* At the lower levels of proficiency, listeners may find short, simple messages easier to process, but students with higher proficiency benefit from the natural redundancy of the language.

— *Does the text involve multiple individuals and objects? Are they clearly differentiated?* It is easier to understand a text with a doctor and a patient than one with two doctors, and it is even easier if they are of the opposite sex. In other words, the more marked the differences, the easier the comprehension.

— *Does the text offer visual support to aid in the interpretation of what the listeners hear?* Visual aids such as maps, diagrams, pictures, or the images in a video help contextualize the listening input and provide clues to meaning.

Use pre-listening activities to prepare students for what they are going to hear or view.

The activities chosen during pre-listening may serve as preparation for listening in several ways. During pre-listening the teacher may

— assess students' background knowledge of the topic and linguistic content of the text

— provide students with the background knowledge necessary for their comprehension of the listening passage or activate the existing knowledge that the students possess

— clarify any cultural information which may be necessary to comprehend the passage

— make students aware of the type of text they will be listening to, the role they will play, and the purpose(s) for which they will be listening

— provide opportunities for group or collaborative work and for background reading or class discussion activities

Sample pre-listening activities:

— looking at pictures, maps, diagrams, or graphs

— reviewing vocabulary or grammatical structures

— reading something relevant

— constructing semantic webs (a graphic arrangement of concepts or words showing how they are related)

— predicting the content of the listening text

— going over the directions or instructions for the activity

— doing guided practice

Match while-listening activities to the instructional goal, the listening purpose, and students' proficiency level.

While-listening activities relate directly to the text, and students do them do during or immediately after the time they are listening. Keep these points in mind when planning while-listening activities:

If students are to complete a written task during or immediately after listening, allow them to read through it before listening. Students need to devote all their attention to the listening task. Be sure they understand the instructions for the written task before listening begins so that they are not distracted by the need to figure out what to do.

Keep writing to a minimum during listening. Remember that the primary goal is comprehension, not production. Having to write while listening may distract students from this primary goal. If a written response is to be given after listening, the task can be more demanding.

Organize activities so that they guide listeners through the text. Combine global activities such as getting the main idea, topic, and setting with selective listening activities that focus on details of content and form.

Use questions to focus students' attention on the elements of the text crucial to comprehension of the whole. Before the listening activity begins, have students review questions they will answer orally or in writing after listening. Listening for the answers will help students recognize the crucial parts of the message.

Use predicting to encourage students to monitor their comprehension as they listen. Do a predicting activity before listening, and remind students to review what they are hearing to see if it makes sense in the context of their prior knowledge and what they already know of the topic or events of the passage.

Give immediate feedback whenever possible. Encourage students to examine how or why their responses were incorrect.

Sample while-listening activities

— listening with visuals

— filling in graphs and charts

— following a route on a map

— checking off items in a list

— listening for the gist

— searching for specific clues to meaning

— completing cloze (fill-in) exercises

— distinguishing between formal and informal registers

Using Textbook Listening Activities

The greatest challenges with textbook tape programs are integrating the listening experiences into classroom instruction and keeping up student interest and motivation. These challenges arise from the fact that most textbook listening programs emphasize product (right or wrong answer) over process (how to get meaning from the selection) and from the fact that the listening activities are usually carried out as an add-on, away from the classroom.

You can use the guidelines for developing listening activities given here as starting points for evaluating and adapting textbook listening programs. At the beginning of the teaching term, orient students to the tape program by completing the exercises in class and discussing the different strategies they use to answer the questions. It is a good idea to periodically complete some of the lab exercises in class to maintain the link to the regular instructional program and to check on the effectiveness of the exercises themselves.

Using Multimedia to Teach Listening

Students can use this outline for both in-class and out-of-class listening/viewing activities. Model and practice the use of the outline at least once in class before you ask students to use it independently.

1. *Plan for listening/viewing*

— Review the vocabulary list, if you have one

— Review the worksheet, if you have one

— Review any information you have about the content of the tape/video

2. *Preview the tape/video*

— (tape) Use fast forward to play segments of the tape; (video) view the video without sound

— Identify the kind of program (news, documentary, interview, drama)

— Make a list of predictions about the content

— Decide how to divide the tape/video into sections for intensive listening/viewing

3. *Listen/view intensively section by section. For each section:*

— Jot down key words you understand

— Answer the worksheet questions pertaining to the section

— If you don't have a worksheet, write a short summary of the section

4. Monitor your comprehension

— Does it fit with the predictions you made?

— Does your summary for each section make sense in relation to the other sections?

5. Evaluate your listening comprehension progress

Assessing Listening Proficiency

You can use post-listening activities to check comprehension, evaluate listening skills and use of listening strategies, and extend the knowledge gained to other contexts. A post-listening activity may relate to a pre-listening activity, such as predicting; may expand on the topic or the language of the listening text; or may transfer what has been learned to reading, speaking, or writing activities.

In order to provide authentic assessment of students' listening proficiency, a post-listening activity must reflect the real-life uses to which students might put information they have gained through listening.

— It must have a purpose other than assessment

— It must require students to demonstrate their level of listening comprehension by completing some task.

To develop authentic assessment activities, consider the type of response that listening to a particular selection would elicit in a non-classroom situation. For example, after listening to a weather report one might decide what to wear the next day; after listening to a set of instructions, one might repeat them to someone else; after watching and listening to a play or video, one might discuss the story line with friends.

Use this response type as a base for selecting appropriate post-listening tasks. You can then develop a checklist or rubric that will allow you to evaluate each student's comprehension of specific parts of the aural text.

For example, for listening practice you have students listen to a weather report. Their purpose for listening is to be able to advise a friend what to wear the next day. As a post-listening activity, you ask students to select appropriate items of clothing from a collection you have assembled, or write a note telling the friend what to wear, or provide oral advice to another student (who has not heard the weather report). To evaluate listening comprehension, you use a checklist containing specific features of the forecast, marking those that are reflected in the student's clothing recommendations.

4

Teaching Speaking

Speaking is an interactive process of constructing meaning that involves producing *and* receiving and processing information. Its form and meaning are dependent on the context in which it occurs, including the participants themselves, their collective experiences, the physical environment, and the purposes for speaking. It is often spontaneous, open-ended, and evolving. However, speech is not always unpredictable. Language functions (or patterns) that tend to recur in certain discourse situations (e.g., declining an invitation or requesting time off from work), can be identified and charted. For example, when a salesperson asks "May I help you?" the expected discourse sequence includes a statement of need, response to the need, offer of appreciation, acknowledgement of the appreciation, and a leave-taking exchange.

Speaking requires that learners not only know how to produce specific points of language such as grammar, pronunciation, or vocabulary *(linguistic competence)*, but also that they understand when, why, and in what ways to produce language *(sociolinguistic competence)*. Finally, speech has its own skills, structures, and conventions different from written language. A good speaker synthesizes this array of skills and knowledge to succeed in a given speech act.

A speaker's skills and speech habits have an impact on the success of any exchange. Speakers must be able to anticipate and then produce the expected patterns of specific discourse situations. They must also manage discrete elements such as turn-taking, rephrasing, providing feedback, or redirecting. For example, a learner involved in the exchange with the salesperson described previously must know the usual pattern that such an interaction follows and access that knowledge as the exchange progresses.

The learner must also choose the correct vocabulary to describe the item sought, rephrase or emphasize words to clarify the description if the clerk does not understand, and use appropriate facial expressions to indicate satisfaction or dissatisfaction with the service. Other skills and knowledge that instruction might address include the following:

— producing the sounds, stress patterns, rhythmic structures, and intonations of the language;

— using grammar structures accurately;

— assessing characteristics of the target audience, including shared knowledge or shared points of reference, status and power relations of participants, interest levels, or differences in perspectives;

— selecting vocabulary that is understandable and appropriate for the audience, the topic being discussed, and the setting in which the speech act occurs;

— applying strategies to enhance comprehensibility, such as emphasizing key words, rephrasing, or checking for listener comprehension;

— using gestures or body language; and

— paying attention to the success of the interaction and adjusting components of speech such as vocabulary, rate of speech, and complexity of grammar structures to maximize listener comprehension and involvement.

Teachers should monitor learners' speech production to determine what skills and knowledge they already have and what areas need development. Bailey and Savage's *New Ways in Teaching Speaking,* and Lewis's *New Ways in Teaching Adults* offer suggestions for activities that can address different skills.

Goal of Teaching Speaking Skills

Many language learners regard speaking ability as the measure of knowing a language. These learners define fluency as the ability to converse with others, much more than the ability to read, write, or comprehend oral language. They regard speaking as the most important skill they can acquire, and they assess their progress in terms of their accomplishments in spoken communication.

Language learners need to recognize that speaking involves three areas of knowledge:

— Mechanics (pronunciation, grammar, and vocabulary): Using the right words in the right order with the correct pronunciation

— Functions (transaction and interaction): Knowing when clarity of message is essential (transaction/information exchange) and when precise understanding is not required (interaction/relationship building)

— Social and cultural rules and norms (turn-taking, rate of speech, length of pauses between speakers, relative roles of participants): Understanding how to take into account who is speaking to whom, in what circumstances, about what, and for what reason.

In the communicative model of language teaching, instructors help their students develop this body of knowledge by providing authentic practice that prepares students for real-life communication situations. They help their students develop the ability to produce grammatically correct, logically connected sentences that are appropriate to specific contexts, and to do so using acceptable (that is, comprehensible) pronunciation.

The goal of teaching speaking skills is communicative efficiency. Learners should be able to make themselves understood, using their current proficiency to the fullest. They should try to avoid confusion in the message due to faulty pronunciation, grammar, or vocabulary, and to observe the social and cultural rules that apply in each communication situation.

To help students develop communicative efficiency in speaking, instructors can use a balanced activities approach that combines language input, structured output, and communicative output.

Language input comes in the form of teacher talk, listening activities, reading passages, and the language heard and read outside of class. It gives learners the material they need to begin producing language themselves.

Language input may be content oriented or form oriented.

— Content-oriented input focuses on information, whether it is a simple weather report or an extended lecture on an academic topic. Content-oriented input may also include descriptions of learning strategies and examples of their use.

— Form-oriented input focuses on ways of using the language: guidance from the teacher or another source on vocabulary, pronunciation, and grammar (linguistic competence); appropriate things to say in specific contexts (discourse competence); expectations for rate of speech, pause length, turn-taking, and other social aspects of language use (sociolinguistic competence); and explicit instruction in phrases to use to ask for clarification and repair miscommunication (strategic competence).

In the presentation part of a lesson, an instructor combines content-oriented and form-oriented input. The amount of input that is actually provided in the target language depends on students' listening proficiency and also on the situation. For students at lower levels, or in situations where a quick explanation on a grammar topic is needed, an explanation in English may be more appropriate than one in the target language.

Structured output focuses on correct form. In structured output, students may have options for responses, but all of the options require them to use the specific form or structure that the teacher has just introduced.

Structured output is designed to make learners comfortable producing specific language items recently introduced, sometimes in combination with previously learned items. Instructors often use structured output exercises as a transition between the presentation stage and the practice stage of a lesson plan. textbook exercises also often make good structured output practice activities.

In communicative output, the learners' main purpose is to complete a task, such as obtaining information, developing a travel plan, or creating a video. To complete the task, they may use the language that the instructor has just presented, but they also may draw on any other vocabulary, grammar, and communication strategies that they know. In communicative output activities, the criterion of success is whether the learner gets the message across. Accuracy is not a consideration unless the lack of it interferes with the message.

In everyday communication, spoken exchanges take place because there is some sort of information gap between the participants. Communicative output activities involve a similar real information gap. In order to complete the task, students must reduce or eliminate the information gap. In these activities, language is a tool, not an end in itself.

In a balanced activities approach, the teacher uses a variety of activities from these different categories of input and output. Learners at all proficiency levels, including beginners, benefit from this variety; it is more motivating, and it is also more likely to result in effective language learning.

Strategies for Developing Speaking Skills

Students often think that the ability to speak a language is the product of language learning, but speaking is also a crucial part of the language learning process. Effective instructors teach students speaking strategies — using minimal responses, recognizing scripts, and using language to talk about language — that they can use to help themselves expand their knowledge of the language and their confidence in using it. These instructors help students learn to speak so that the students can use speaking to learn.

1. Using Minimal Responses

Language learners who lack confidence in their ability to participate successfully in oral interaction often listen in silence while others do the talking. One way to encourage such learners to begin to participate is to help them build up a stock of minimal responses that they can use in different types of exchanges. Such responses can be especially useful for beginners.

Minimal responses are predictable, often idiomatic phrases that conversation participants use to indicate understanding, agreement, doubt, and other responses to what another speaker is saying. Having a stock of such responses enables a learner to focus on what the other participant is saying, without having to simultaneously plan a response.

2. Recognizing Scripts

Some communication situations are associated with a predictable set of spoken exchanges — a script. Greetings, apologies, compliments, invitations, and other functions that are influenced by social and cultural norms often follow patterns or scripts. So do the transactional exchanges involved in activities such as obtaining information and making a purchase. In these scripts, the relationship between a speaker's turn and the one that follows it can often be anticipated.

Instructors can help students develop speaking ability by making them aware of the scripts for different situations so that they can predict what they will hear and what they will need to say in response. Through interactive activities, instructors can give students practice in managing and varying the language that different scripts contain.

3. Using Language to Talk about Language

Language learners are often too embarrassed or shy to say anything when they do not understand another speaker or when they realize that a conversation partner has not understood them. Instructors can help students overcome this reticence by assuring them that misunderstanding and the need for clarification can occur in any type of interaction, whatever the participants' language skill levels. Instructors can also give students strategies and phrases to use for clarification and comprehension check.

By encouraging students to use clarification phrases in class when misunderstanding occurs, and by responding positively when they do, instructors can create an authentic practice environment within the classroom itself. As they develop control of various clarification strategies, students will gain confidence in their ability to manage the various communication situations that they may encounter outside the classroom.

Improving Oral Communication Skills

Communicative and whole language instructional approaches promote integration of speaking, listening, reading, and writing in ways that reflect natural language use. But opportunities for speaking and listening require structure and planning if they are to support language development.

Outside the classroom

Outside the classroom, listening is used twice as often as speaking, which in turn is used twice as much as reading and writing. Inside the classroom, speaking and listening are the most often used skills . These skills are also logical instructional starting points when learners have low literacy levels or limited formal education, or when they come from language backgrounds with a non-Roman script or a predominantly oral tradition. Further, with the drive to incorporate workforce readiness skills into adult instruction, practice time is being devoted to such speaking skills as reporting, negotiating, clarifying, and problem solving.

General outline of a speaking lesson

Speaking lessons can follow the usual pattern of preparation, presentation, practice, evaluation, and extension.

The teacher can use the *preparation* step to establish a context for the speaking task (where, when, why, and with whom it will occur) and to initiate awareness of the speaking skill to be targeted (asking for clarification, stressing key words, using reduced forms of words).

In *presentation*, the teacher can provide learners with a preproduction model that furthers learner comprehension and helps them become more attentive observers of language use.

Practice involves learners in reproducing the targeted structure, usually in a controlled or highly supported manner.

Evaluation involves directing attention to the skill being examined and asking learners to monitor and assess their own progress. Finally, *extension* consists of activities that ask learners to use the strategy or skill in a different context or authentic communicative situation, or to integrate use of the new skill or strategy with previously acquired ones.

Choosing appropriate topics for small talk

1. *Preparation.* Show the learners a picture of two people conversing in a familiar casual setting. (The setting will be determined by a prior needs assessment.) Ask them to brainstorm what the people might be discussing (i.e., what topics, vocabulary, typical phrases).

2. *Presentation.* Present several video clips of small talk in casual situations. Have learners complete a worksheet in which they describe or list the topics discussed, the context in which the speech is occurring, and any phrases that seem to typify small talk. Follow up with a discussion of the kinds of topics that are appropriate for small talk, the factors in the specific situations that affect topic selection (e.g., relationships of participants, physical setting), and typical phrases used in small talk. Chart this information.

3. *Practice.* Give learners specific information about the participants and the setting of a scenario where small talk will take place. In pairs, have them list topics that might be discussed by the participants and simple phrases they might use. Learners then engage in improvised dialogues based on these simple phrases.

4. *Evaluation.* Give pairs a teacher-prepared dialogue based on their scenario from. Ask them to compare their improvised dialogues with the prepared dialogue, analyzing the similarities, differences, and reasons for both.

5. *Extension.* Have learners go individually or in small groups into various contexts in the community and record the conversations they hear. Ask them to report their findings back to the class, and then have the class discuss these findings.

In-class speaking tasks

Although dialogues and conversations are the most obvious and most often used speaking activities in language classrooms, a teacher can select activities from a variety of tasks. Brown lists six possible task categories:

— *Imitative:*Drills in which the learner simply repeats a phrase or structure (e.g., "Excuse me." or "Can you help me?") for clarity and accuracy;

— *Intensive:* Drills or repetitions focusing on specific phonological or grammatical points, such as minimal pairs or repetition of a series of imperative sentences;

— *Responsive:* Short replies to teacher or learner questions or comments, such as a series of answers to yes/no questions;

— *Transactional:* Dialogues conducted for the purpose of information exchange, such as information-gathering interviews, role plays, or debates;

— *Interpersonal:* Dialogues to establish or maintain social relationships, such as personal interviews or casual conversation role plays; and

— *Extensive:* Extended monologues such as short speeches, oral reports, or oral summaries.

These tasks are not sequential. Each can be used independently or they can be integrated with one another, depending on learners' needs. For example, if learners are not using appropriate sentence intonations when participating in a *transactional* activity that focuses on the skill of politely interrupting to make a point, the teacher might decide to follow up with a brief *imitative* lesson targeting this feature.

When presenting tasks, teachers should tell learners about the language function to be produced in the task and the real context(s) in which it usually occurs. They should provide opportunities for interactive practice and build upon previous instruction as necessary. Teachers should also be careful not to overload a speaking lesson with other new material such as numerous vocabulary or grammatical structures. This can distract learners from the primary speaking goals of the lesson.

Developing Speaking Activities

Traditional classroom speaking practice often takes the form of drills in which one person asks a question and another gives an answer. The question and the answer are structured and predictable, and often there is only one correct, predetermined answer. The purpose of asking and answering the question is to demonstrate the ability to ask and answer the question.

In contrast, the purpose of real communication is to accomplish a task, such as conveying a telephone message, obtaining information, or expressing an opinion. In real communication, participants must manage uncertainty about what the other person will say. Authentic communication involves an information gap; each participant has information that the other does not have. In addition, to achieve their purpose, participants may have to clarify their meaning or ask for confirmation of their own understanding.

To create classroom speaking activities that will develop communicative competence, instructors need to incorporate a purpose and an information gap and allow for multiple forms of expression. However, quantity alone will not necessarily produce competent speakers. Instructors need to combine structured output activities, which allow for error correction and increased accuracy, with communicative output activities that give students opportunities to practice language use more freely.

Structured Output Activities

Two common kinds of structured output activities are *information gap* and *jigsaw* activities. In both these types of activities, students complete a task by obtaining missing information, a feature the activities have in common with real communication. However, information gap and jigsaw activities also set up practice on specific items of language. In this respect they are more like drills than like communication.

The aim of speaking is communication and that does not require perfect language, then it makes sense to encourage quantity in your classroom. Break the silence and get students communicating with whatever language they can use, correct or not, and selectively address errors that block communication.

Speaking lessons often tie in pronunciation and grammar which are necessary for effective oral communication. Or a grammar or reading lesson may incorporate a speaking activity. Either way, your students will need some preparation before the speaking task. This includes introducing the topic and providing a model of the speech they are to produce. A model may not apply to discussion-type activities, in which case students will need clear and specific instructions about the task to be accomplished. Then the students will practice with the actual speaking activity.

These activities may include imitating (repeating), answering verbal cues, interactive conversation, or an oral presentation. Most speaking activities inherently practice listening skills as well, such as when one student is given a simple drawing and sits behind another student, facing away. The first must give instructions to the second to reproduce the drawing. The second student asks questions to clarify unclear instructions, and neither can look at each other's page during the activity. Information gaps are also commonly used for speaking practice, as are surveys, discussions, and role-plays. Speaking activities abound; see the Activities and Further Resources sections of this guide for ideas.

Here are some ideas to keep in mind as you plan your speaking activities.

— *Content*: As much as possible, the content should be practical and usable in real-life situations. Avoid too much new vocabulary or grammar, and focus on speaking with the language the students have.

— *Correcting Errors*: You need to provide appropriate feedback and correction, but don't interrupt the flow of communication. Take notes while pairs or groups are talking and address problems to the class after the activity without embarrassing the student who made the error. You can write the error on the board and ask who can correct it.

— *Quantity vs. Quality*: Address both interactive fluency and accuracy, striving foremost for communication. Get to know each learner's personality and encourage the quieter ones to take more risks.

— *Conversation Strategies*: Encourage strategies like asking for clarification, paraphrasing, gestures, and initiating ('hey,' 'so,' 'by the way').

— Teacher Intervention: If a speaking activity loses steam, you may need to jump into a role-play, ask more discussion questions, clarify your instructions, or stop an activity that is too difficult or boring.

Information Gap Activities

— *Filling the gaps in a schedule or timetable*: Partner A holds an airline timetable with some of the arrival and departure times missing. Partner B has the same timetable but with different blank spaces. The two partners are not permitted to see each other's timetables and must fill in the blanks by asking each other appropriate questions. The features of language that are practiced would include questions beginning with "when" or "at what time." Answers would be limited mostly to time expressions like "at 8:15" or "at ten in the evening."

— *Completing the picture*: The two partners have similar pictures, each with different missing details, and they cooperate to find all the missing details. In another variation, no items are missing, but similar items differ in appearance. For example, in one picture, a man walking along the street may be wearing an overcoat, while in the other the man is wearing a jacket. The features of grammar and vocabulary that are practiced are determined by the content of the pictures and the items that are missing or different. Differences in the activities depicted lead to practice of different verbs. Differences in number, size, and shape lead to adjective practice. Differing locations would probably be described with prepositional phrases.

These activities may be set up so that the partners must practice more than just grammatical and lexical features. For example, the timetable activity gains a social dimension when one partner assumes the role of a student trying to make an appointment with a partner who takes the role of a professor. Each partner has pages from an appointment book in which certain dates and times are already filled in and other times are still available for an appointment. Of course, the open times don't match exactly, so there must be some polite negotiation to arrive at a mutually convenient time for a meeting or a conference.

Jigsaw Activities

Jigsaw activities are more elaborate information gap activities that can be done with several partners. In a jigsaw activity, each partner has one or a few pieces of the "puzzle," and the partners must cooperate to fit all the pieces into a whole picture. The puzzle piece may take one of several forms. It may be one panel from a comic strip or one photo from a set that tells a story. It may be one sentence from a written narrative. It may be a tape recording of a conversation, in which case no two partners hear exactly the same conversation.

In one fairly simple jigsaw activity, students work in groups of four. Each student in the group receives one panel from a comic strip. Partners may not show each other their panels. Together the four panels present this narrative: a man takes a container of ice cream from the freezer; he serves himself several scoops of ice cream; he sits in front of the TV eating his ice cream; he returns with the empty bowl to the kitchen and finds that he left the container of ice cream, now melting, on the kitchen counter. These pictures have a clear narrative line and the partners are not likely to disagree about the appropriate sequencing. You can make the task more demanding, however, by using pictures that lend themselves to alternative sequences, so that the partners have to negotiate among themselves to agree on a satisfactory sequence.

More elaborate jigsaws may proceed in two stages. Students first work in input groups (groups A, B, C, and D) to receive information. Each group receives a different part of the total information for the task. Students then reorganize into groups of four with one student each from A, B, C, and D, and use the information they received to complete the task. Such an organization could be used, for example, when the input is given in the form of a tape recording. Groups A, B, C, and D each hear a different recording of a short news bulletin. The four recordings all contain the same general information, but each has one or more details that the others do not. In the second stage, students reconstruct the complete story by comparing the four versions.

With information gap and jigsaw activities, instructors need to be conscious of the language demands they place on their students. If an activity calls for language your students have not already practiced, you can brainstorm with them when setting up the activity to preview the language they will need, eliciting what they already know and supplementing what they are able to produce themselves.

Structured output activities can form an effective bridge between instructor modeling and communicative output because they are partly authentic and partly artificial. Like authentic communication, they feature information gaps that must be bridged for successful completion of the task.

However, where authentic communication allows speakers to use all of the language they know, structured output activities lead students to practice specific features of language and to practice only in brief sentences, not in extended discourse. Also, structured output situations are contrived and more like games than real communication, and the participants' social roles are irrelevant to the performance of the activity. This structure controls the number of variables that students must deal with when they are first exposed to new material. As they become comfortable, they can move on to true communicative output activities.

Communicative Output Activities

Communicative output activities allow students to practice using all of the language they know in situations that resemble real settings. In these activities, students must work together to develop a plan, resolve a problem, or complete a task. The most common types of communicative output activity are *role plays* and *discussions* .

In role plays, students are assigned roles and put into situations that they may eventually encounter outside the classroom. Because role plays imitate life, the range of language functions that may be used expands considerably. Also, the role relationships among the students as they play their parts call for them to practice and develop their sociolinguistic competence. They have to use language that is appropriate to the situation and to the characters.

Students usually find role playing enjoyable, but students who lack self-confidence or have lower proficiency levels may find them intimidating at first. To succeed with role plays:

— *Prepare carefully:* Introduce the activity by describing the situation and making sure that all of the students understand it

— *Set a goal or outcome*: Be sure the students understand what the product of the role play should be, whether a plan, a schedule, a group opinion, or some other product

— *Use role cards:* Give each student a card that describes the person or role to be played. For lower-level students, the cards can include words or expressions that that person might use.

— *Brainstorm:* Before you start the role play, have students brainstorm as a class to predict what vocabulary, grammar, and idiomatic expressions they might use.

— *Keep groups small:* Less-confident students will feel more able to participate if they do not have to compete with many voices.

— *Give students time to prepare*: Let them work individually to outline their ideas and the language they will need to express them.

— *Be present as a resource, not a monitor:* Stay in communicative mode to answer students' questions. Do not correct their pronunciation or grammar unless they specifically ask you about it.

— *Allow students to work at their own levels*: Each student has individual language skills, an individual approach to working in groups, and a specific role to play in the activity. Do not expect all students to contribute equally to the discussion, or to use every grammar point you have taught.

— *Do topical follow-up:* Have students report to the class on the outcome of their role plays.

— *Do linguistic follow-up:* After the role play is over, give feedback on grammar or pronunciation problems you have heard. This can wait until another class period when you plan to review pronunciation or grammar anyway.

— Discussions, like role plays, succeed when the instructor prepares students first, and then gets out of the way. To succeed with discussions:

— *Prepare the students:* Give them input (both topical information and language forms) so that they will have something to say and the language with which to say it.

— *Offer choices:* Let students suggest the topic for discussion or choose from several options. Discussion does not always have to be about serious issues. Students are likely to be more motivated to participate if the topic is television programs, plans for a vacation, or news about mutual friends. Weighty topics like how to combat pollution are not as engaging and place heavy demands on students' linguistic competence.

— *Set a goal or outcome*: This can be a group product, such as a letter to the editor, or individual reports on the views of others in the group.

— *Use small groups instead of whole-class discussion:* Large groups can make participation difficult.

— *Keep it short*: Give students a defined period of time, not more than 8-10 minutes, for discussion. Allow them to stop sooner if they run out of things to say.

— *Allow students to participate in their own way:* Not every student will feel comfortable talking about every topic. Do not expect all of them to contribute equally to the conversation.

Through well-prepared communicative output activities such as role plays and discussions, you can encourage students to experiment and innovate with the language, and create a supportive atmosphere that allows them to make mistakes without fear of embarrassment. This will contribute to their self-confidence as speakers and to their motivation to learn more.

Teaching Speaking: Suggestions for the Classroom

In speaking classes students must be exposed to three key items:

(1) form-focused instruction, that is, attention to details of pronunciation, grammar, vocabulary, and so forth;

(2) meaning-focused instruction, that is, opportunities to produce meaningful spoken messages with real communicative purposes; and

(3) opportunities to improve fluency. Elements of all of the above should be present throughout a speaking program, with emphasis on form-focused instruction at the elementary levels and, as the learners progress, on meaning-focused instruction at the higher levels.

Form-Focused Speaking

When learners first begin to speak in another language their speaking will need to be based on some form-focused learning. An effective way to begin is to base speaking on some useful, simple memorized phrases and sentences. These may be greetings, simple personal descriptions, and simple questions and answers. These can be practiced in Repetition drills. The teacher says a phrase or sentence several times and then asks the learners to repeat. Some learners can be called on to repeat individually, and then the class may repeat together. Because it is helpful to give learners quite a lot of repetition practice in beginning level courses, the teacher needs to find ways of varying repetition activities to keep the learners interested. Here is a list of possible ways to vary repetition. As an example, use the sentence "Where is the train station?"

1. *The teacher varies the speed.* The teacher says the sentence slowly and the learners repeat. Then the teacher says the phrase a little faster until the phrase is being said at normal speaking speed.

2. The teacher varies the way of choosing who is to repeat the sentence. The teacher says the sentence and points to the first person in the first row to repeat it. The teacher says it again and points to the second person in the first row. Then the teacher starts pointing at people at random so that the learners cannot predict who will be the next person called on. This variation can also include choosing individuals or choosing the whole class to repeat the sentence. Another variation of this kind is to get the learner who just repeated the sentence to call the name of the next person to repeat the sentence.

3. The teacher can vary the content of the sentence. That is, the teacher can substitute a word for one of the words in a sentence. So instead of only saying "Where is the train station?" the learners might also be called on to repeat "Where is the Post Office?" This is called a Substitution drill.

4. The teacher varies the way the substitution is signaled to the learners, for example, on the board there may be a substitution table like this:

Where is

— the station?

— the post office?

— your house?

— the bank?

— the hospital?

At first the teacher points to the words "the station" on the board and says "Where is the station?" The learners repeat. The teacher points to the next substitution, "the post office," and says that and the learners repeat. After doing this for a while, the teacher just points to the substitution and does not say it, but the learners have to say the whole sentence. After doing that for a while the teacher does not point but just says the substitution.

5. The teacher may vary the way of choosing the substitution. At first, the teacher chooses the substitutions in the same order as they are written on the board. Then the teacher may choose them in random order so that the learners cannot predict what the next substitution will be.

The Role of Drills

The skill of a teacher in carrying out a drill lies in learning when to vary the activity so that the learners do not become bored by it. Skilled teachers make continual, small variations so that the activity is always challenging, smooth, and interesting. The activity can be taken a step towards a more meaning-focused activity by getting the learners to choose their own words to substitute for words in the model sentence.

The 1970s saw the first steps away from (among other teacher-centered approaches) audiolingualism, a method of teaching that sees the role of the teacher as "central and active . . . [who] provides models, controls direction and pace". In this methodology, teacher-centered drill activities play a large role in the curriculum. With the rise recently of more student-centered approaches — ''which are characterized by the involvement of the learner, and the utilization of information about the learner in all aspects of the curriculum" — repetition and substitution drills have come to be considered old-fashioned and (worse still) not useful for language learning.

While acknowledging the contribution that audiolingualism has made, Stern essentially argues against its use: "It's theoretical base was found to be weak. But also in practical terms its hopes had not been fulfilled. Empirical research did not conclusively establish its superiority, and teachers using audiolingual materials . . . complained about the lack of effectiveness of the techniques in the long run and the boredom they engendered among the students" . Moreover, on the role of the teacher in the classroom, Widdowson writes: "It is widely accepted that is undesirable to force learning into conformity with the teacher's preconceived ideas, and it is preferable for the teacher to adapt to the learner rather than the reverse".

The use of drills, however, should be seen as merely one kind of form-focused activity that needs to be balanced with other types of form-focused activities, as well as with meaning-focused and fluency development activities. Drills play a useful part in a language course in helping learners to be formally accurate in their speech and in helping them to quickly learn a useful collection of phrases and sentences that allow them to start using the language as soon as possible. As their proficiency and experience in the language develop, most of these sentences and phrases may be re-analyzed and incorporated into the learners' system of knowledge of the language. Language use based on memorization can be the starting point for more creative use of the language.

Meaning-Focused Speaking

In addition to form-focused speaking, language learners should also be exposed to and given opportunities to practice and use meaning-focused communication, in which they must both produce and listen to meaningful oral communication. An example of a meaning-focused activity for beginning students is Speaking by numbers. Each learner is given a number and a topic. The topics could include family, money, coming to school, a color, future goals, travel, work, and so forth. The learners can think about their topics for a minute or two and then the teacher calls a number. The learner with that number then says two or three sentences about his or her particular topic. The speaker then calls a number and the learner with that number has to ask the speaker a question or two related to the topic just spoken about. When the question is answered, the questioner calls a number and the person with that number asks another question. This continues three or four times and then the speaker calls the number of a new person who will speak about the topic that she or he was given.

This is a meaning-focused speaking activity because both the speaker's and the listeners' attention is on the message being communicated.

Developing the Learner's Knowledge of Language Items

A problem in meaning-focused speaking activities is making sure that the activity is actually developing the learner's knowledge of language items. There are several ways of using speaking to increase the speaker's control of the language items.

1. The meaning-focused speaking activity follows some form-focused instruction. That is, the teacher presents some new vocabulary or grammatical features, gives the learners some practice, and then uses a meaning-focused activity to help the learners use and remember these items.

2. Before the learners speak on a topic or take part in an activity, they work in pairs or groups of three of four to prepare. This gives the learners the chance to learn new items from each other. Here is an example using a Same or different information gap activity. In this kind of activity the learners work in pairs. Learner A has a set of small numbered pictures. Learner B has a similar set except that while some of B's are exactly the same as A's, some are different. They should sit facing each other so that they cannot see each other's picture(s). Learner A describes the first picture and B listens and then says if her picture is the same or different. If it is the same they both write S next to their picture; if it is different they both write D. Then Learner B describes picture number 2 and they decide if the pictures are the same or different. After they have done five or ten pictures, they can change partners so that Learner A works with a new Learner B. Before the activity begins, all the Learner As can get together in groups and help each other describe their pictures. All the Learner Bs do the same. When they have had enough preparation and practice they form Learner A and B pairs and do the activity.

3. The learners are given topics to talk about. They prepare at home, using dictionaries, reference texts, reading sources, and so forth. Here is an example called Newspaper talks. Each learner has to choose a short and interesting article from an English language newspaper to present to the class. The learner must not read the article aloud to the class but must describe the main points of the article. The class should then ask the presenter questions.

4. Many speaking activities involve some kind of written or picture input in the form of a worksheet. In the Same or different activity this is two sheets of pictures. In a Ranking activity or a Problem Solving activity, the worksheet contains written data about the situation, what to do, and possible choices. In a "Who Gets the Heart" activity, for example, a group of three or four students must decide from a list of several possible candidates who is to receive the only available heart for transplantation. None of the patients will survive without the new heart. They are a Nobel Prize winner in medical research (a 59 year old male with no family), a homemaker of three (32 year old female), an Olympic athlete (24 year old female, married with no children), an Academy award winning film director (female, 37 years old, two children), and a 45 year old homeless male. The students must rank in order which of these people is most deserving of the heart. Then, each student presents his/her case to the group. Based on these presentations, and the ensuing discussion, the group must choose one candidate for the transplant. Then, each group must present its conclusion to the class as a whole.

   The worksheets contain vocabulary and phrases that may be new to the learners and which will be necessary or useful in the speaking activity. For example, in the Ranking activity, the vocabulary in the list of items to rank will need to be used by the learners. Those items which generate the most disagreement over the ranking will likely result in the greatest amount of vocabulary learning. According to Joe, Nation and Newton: "Negotiation of word meaning indicates that an item is noticed and that the learner has a gap in his or her knowledge. Items which [are] negotiated [have] a much greater chance of being learned than items which were not negotiated". If the teacher gives careful thought to the placement of new vocabulary in worksheets for speaking activities, there is a very good chance that the vocabulary will be learned during the speaking activity. If the worksheet uses pictures, some of the pictures or parts of pictures can be given labels that can be used in describing the pictures.

5. Some speaking activities encourage learners to ask each other about the meaning of unfamiliar words or constructions. This seeking and giving of explanations is called negotiation. There are similarities between this type of activity and the Same or Different activity in that each learner in a pair or group has different pieces of information for completing the activity. These kinds of activities are given lots of different names including jigsaw tasks, two-way tasks, information gap, and so forth.

We have looked at five different ways of making meaning-focused speaking tasks contribute to a learner's knowledge of language items. Language can be learned through production (speaking and writing) as well as through reception (listening and reading), but this learning needs to be planned.

Development of Speaking Fluency

Fluency in speaking is the aim of many language learners. Signs of fluency include a reasonably fast speed of speaking and only a small number of pauses and "ums" and "ers." These signs indicate that the speaker does not have to spend a lot of time searching for the language items needed to express the message.

4/3/2 is a useful technique for developing fluency and includes the features that are needed in fluency development activities. First the learners choose a topic or are given a topic with which they are very familiar. The first time that learners use this technique it may be best if the topic involves recounting something that happened to them. This is because the chronological order of the events will make it easier to recall and repeat because the time sequence provides a clear structure for the talk. The learners work in pairs. Learner A tells a story to Learner B and has a time limit of four minutes to do this. B just listens and does not interrupt or question Learner A. When the four minutes are up, the teacher says, "Change partners"; learner A then moves to a new Learner B. The teacher says "Begin" and Learner A tells exactly the same story to the new partner but this time has only three minutes to tell it. When the three minutes are up, the teacher says "Stop. Change partners." With a new partner, Learner A now has two minutes to tell the story. During the three deliveries of the same story, the B learners do not talk and each listens to three different people. When the A learners have given their talk three times, the B learners can now go through the same sequence, this time as speakers.

Research on this activity shows that the learners' speed of speaking increased during the talks (as measured by the number of words per minute), the hesitations they make decrease (as measured by hesitations per 100 words), and surprisingly their grammatical errors in the repeated parts of the talk decrease and they tend to use several, more complex grammatical constructions in the last of the three talks than they did in the first talk.

The features in 4/3/2 that help the development of fluency are the same features that occur in activities to develop listening fluency.

— The activity involves known vocabulary, grammar, and discourse.

— The learners have a high chance of performing successfully at a higher than normal speed.

— There are repeated opportunities to do the same thing.

— Here are other techniques to develop speaking fluency that involve the same features.

In the Headlines activity, students create newspaper "headlines" that will serve as the basis for the speaking activity. The learners all think of an interesting or exciting thing that has happened to them. Using a felt-tipped pen — so that the writing is easily seen — each learner writes a newspaper headline referring to that event.

The teacher should give some examples to help the learners, such as "Burning Bed Brings Joy" and "Forgotten Shoes Never Return." Half of the learners hold their headlines up for the rest of the class to see. Those not holding up a headline go to hear a story behind the headline that interests them. Each story can be told to no more than two people at a time. When the story is done, the listeners should circulate to a second headline that interests them. The tellers will thus have to repeat their story several times. After there has been plenty of opportunity to tell the stories, the other half of the class hold up their headlines and, in similar fashion, tell their stories.

4/3/2 and Headlines rely on repetition of the same story to develop fluency. This kind of fluency is useful for predictable topics that learners may need to speak about. For example, when meeting other people learners may need to talk about themselves, about their country, about the kind of food they eat, about their travels, about their interests and hobbies, and about their experiences. Speaking fluency also needs to be developed for less predictable topics and the Say it! activity is a useful way of doing this.

In Say it!, learners work in groups of about four people. First they read a Say it! text carefully until they have reached a good understanding of it. They discuss their understanding of the text to make sure everything is fairly clear. Then they do the tasks in the Say it! grid, which is a collection of simple verbal tasks related to the reading. One learner chooses a square for the next learner to perform, for example square B2. The learner does this task while the others observe and, when the student has finished, s/he calls a square, for example, A3, for the next learner. This continues with some learners doing the same task several times and with some tasks being done several times by different learners.

Often the tasks are like role plays and require the learners to use the vocabulary that was in the reading text, but to use it in a different way. This helps the development of fluency by providing lots of associations with the vocabulary used in the task, that is the associations from the reading text and its discussion, and the associations from the Say it! role play. Although the Say it! activity does not involve large amounts of repetition, it involves preparation by the learners. That is, the learners prepare for the spoken task by studying the written text. This preparation should increase the fluency with which learners do the spoken task.

Error Correction

Some learners may experience difficulty in pronouncing certain sounds and groups of sounds in another language. Some Chinese and Japanese speakers of English, for example, have trouble with /l/ and /r/. Some learners have trouble with the beginning sounds in the words "three" and "they:" Giving too much attention to the correction of pronunciation in the early stages of language learning can make learners worried and reluctant to speak because of fear of making errors.

It is worth thinking about why errors occur, because this can help teachers decide what to do about them. The study of errors and their causes is called error analysis.

For each cause listed below, suggestions for the teacher are given in square brackets.

1. The learner makes an error because the learner has not had sufficient chance to observe the correct form or to develop sufficient knowledge of the language system. [Don't correct the learner but give more models and opportunities to observe.]

2. The learner makes an error because the learner has not observed the form correctly. [Give a little correction by showing the learner the difference between the correct form and the learner's error.]

3. The learner makes an error because of nervousness. [Don't correct. Use less threatening activities — or, if and when appropriate, joke with the person/class/ yourself to lighten the mood.]

4. The learner makes an error because the activity is difficult, that is, there are many things the learner has to think about during the activity. This is sometimes called cognitive overload. [Don't correct. Make the activity easier or give several chances to repeat the activity.]

5. The learner makes an error because the activity is confusing. Use of tongue twisters, for instance, for pronunciation can be confusing. [Don't correct. Improve the activity.]

6. The learner makes an error because the learner is using patterns from the first language instead of the patterns from the second language. [Give some correction. If there has been plenty of opportunity to develop knowledge of the second language, then some time should be spent on correction to help the learner break out of making errors that are unlikely to change. Errors which are resistant to change are sometimes called fossilized errors and imaginative correction is often needed to break the fossilization. If there has not been a lot of opportunity to develop knowledge of the second language, correct by telling the learner what to look for when observing people using the second language. This is called consciousness raising. It does not actually teach the correct form but makes the learner more aware of what to look for to learn it.]

7. The learner makes an error because the learner has been copying incorrect models. [Correct the learner and provide better models.]

This range of causes shows that the teacher should not rush into error correction, but should consider whether the error is worth the interruption and, if it is, the teacher should consider possible causes and then think of appropriate ways of dealing with the error.

Pronunciation Correction

The teaching and correcting of pronunciation to learners who are past the age of puberty is often a difficult task. The audiolingualism method argues that native-like pronunciation is one of the most important aspects of language proficiency. However, as Ueno reports: "The research on this issue [whether specific instruction can improve students' pronunciation] is inconclusive. In a recent survey . . . almost half of the recent experiments on this subject show no improvement in students' production of target-language sounds". There is some hope that specific pronunciation instruction may be effective in improving students' perception or overall comprehension of the target-language. Moreover, to use a sports metaphor, a beginning tennis player must "develop and automatize basic muscle skills necessary to perform the new physical tasks. Similarly, a language learner must practice the new motor skills involved in producing the sounds of the target language".

The following are simple suggestions for correcting pronunciation.

1. Say "What?" and see if the learner is capable of self-correction.

2. Give the correct form for the learner to copy. If the learner cannot copy it after two or three attempts, then some explanation and guidance may be needed.

3. Explain how to make the correct form and, if necessary, what is wrong with the error. For example, to make the /th/ sound as in "then," say "Put your tongue between your teeth and make a long sound." A

variation on this is to tell the learner to look at what you are doing and say, "Put your tongue like this."

Assessing Speaking

Speaking assessments can take many forms, from oral sections of standardized tests to authentic assessments such as progress checklists, analysis of taped speech samples, or anecdotal records of speech in classroom interactions. Assessment instruments should reflect instruction and be incorporated from the beginning stages of lesson planning . For example, if a lesson focuses on producing and recognizing signals for turn-taking in a group discussion, the assessment tool might be a checklist to be completed by the teacher or learners in the course of the learners' participation in the discussion. Finally, criteria should be clearly defined and understandable to both the teacher and the learners.

5

Teaching Reading

Traditionally, the purpose of learning to read in a language has been to have access to the literature written in that language. In language instruction, reading materials have traditionally been chosen from literary texts that represent "higher" forms of culture.

This approach assumes that students learn to read a language by studying its vocabulary, grammar, and sentence structure, not by actually reading it. In this approach, lower level learners read only sentences and paragraphs generated by textbook writers and instructors. The reading of authentic materials is limited to the works of great authors and reserved for upper level students who have developed the language skills needed to read them.

The communicative approach to language teaching has given instructors a different understanding of the role of reading in the language classroom and the types of texts that can be used in instruction. When the goal of instruction is communicative competence, everyday materials such as train schedules, newspaper articles, and travel and tourism Web sites become appropriate classroom materials, because reading them is one way communicative competence is developed. Instruction in reading and reading practice thus become essential parts of language teaching at every level.

Purpose of Reading

Reading is an activity with a purpose. A person may read in order to gain information or verify existing knowledge, or in order to critique a writer's ideas or writing style. A person may also read for enjoyment, or to enhance knowledge of the language being read. The purpose(s) for reading guide the reader's selection of texts.

The purpose for reading also determines the appropriate approach to reading comprehension. A person who needs to know whether she can afford to eat at a particular restaurant needs to comprehend the pricing information provided on the menu, but does not need to recognize the name of every appetizer listed. A person reading poetry for enjoyment needs to recognize the words the poet uses and the ways they are put together, but does not need to identify main idea and supporting details. However, a person using a scientific article to support an opinion needs to know the vocabulary that is used, understand the facts and cause-effect sequences that are presented, and recognize ideas that are presented as hypotheses and givens.

Reading research shows that good readers

— Read extensively

— Integrate information in the text with existing knowledge

— Have a flexible reading style, depending on what they are reading

— Are motivated

— Rely on different skills interacting: perceptual processing, phonemic processing, recall

— Read for a purpose; reading serves a function

Reading as a Process

Reading is an interactive process that goes on between the reader and the text, resulting in comprehension. The text presents letters, words, sentences, and paragraphs that encode meaning. The reader uses knowledge, skills, and strategies to determine what that meaning is.

Reader knowledge, skills, and strategies include

- Linguistic competence: the ability to recognize the elements of the writing system; knowledge of vocabulary; knowledge of how words are structured into sentences
- Discourse competence: knowledge of discourse markers and how they connect parts of the text to one another
- Sociolinguistic competence: knowledge about different types of texts and their usual structure and content
- Strategic competence: the ability to use top-down strategies as well as knowledge of the language (a bottom-up strategy)

The purpose(s) for reading and the type of text determine the specific knowledge, skills, and strategies that readers need to apply to achieve comprehension. Reading comprehension is thus much more than decoding. Reading comprehension results when the reader knows which skills and strategies are appropriate for the type of text, and understands how to apply them to accomplish the reading purpose.

Goals of Teaching Reading

Instructors want to produce students who, even if they do not have complete control of the grammar or an extensive lexicon, can fend for themselves in communication situations. In the case of reading, this means producing students who can use reading strategies to maximize their comprehension of text, identify relevant and non-relevant information, and tolerate less than word-by-word comprehension.

To accomplish this goal, instructors focus on the process of reading rather than on its product.

- They develop students' awareness of the reading process and reading strategies by asking students to think and talk about how they read in their native language.
- They allow students to practice the full repertoire of reading strategies by using authentic reading tasks. They encourage students to read to learn (and have an authentic purpose for reading) by giving students some choice of reading material.
- When working with reading tasks in class, they show students the strategies that will work best for the reading purpose and the type of text. They explain how and why students should use the strategies.
- They have students practice reading strategies in class and ask them to practice outside of class in their reading assignments. They encourage students to be conscious of what they're doing while they complete reading assignments.
- They encourage students to evaluate their comprehension and self-report their use of strategies.

They build comprehension checks into in-class and out-of-class reading assignments, and periodically review how and when to use particular strategies.

— They encourage the development of reading skills and the use of reading strategies by using the target language to convey instructions and course-related information in written form: office hours, homework assignments, test content.

— They do not assume that students will transfer strategy use from one task to another. They explicitly mention how a particular strategy can be used in a different type of reading task or with another skill.

By raising students' awareness of reading as a skill that requires active engagement, and by explicitly teaching reading strategies, instructors help their students develop both the ability and the confidence to handle communication situations they may encounter beyond the classroom. In this way they give their students the foundation for communicative competence in the new language.

Integrating Reading Strategies

Instruction in reading strategies is not an add-on, but rather an integral part of the use of reading activities in the language classroom. Instructors can help their students become effective readers by teaching them how to use strategies before, during, and after reading.

Plan for the Reading task

— Set a purpose or decide in advance what to read for

— Decide if more linguistic or background knowledge is needed

— Determine whether to enter the text from the top down (attend to the overall meaning) or from the bottom up (focus on the words and phrases)

Monitor Comprehension

— Verify predictions and check for inaccurate guesses

— Decide what is and is not important to understand

— Reread to check comprehension

— Ask for help

Evaluate Comprehension and Strategy Use

— Evaluate comprehension in a particular task or area

— Evaluate overall progress in reading and in particular types of reading tasks

— Decide if the strategies used were appropriate for the purpose and for the task

— Modify strategies if necessary

Learning about a Text before Really Reading It

Previewing enables readers to get a sense of what the text is about and how it is organized before reading it closely. This simple strategy includes seeing what you can learn from the headnotes or other introductory material, skimming to get an overview of the content and organization, and identifying the rhetorical situation.

Placing a Text in its Historical, Biographical, and Cultural Contexts

When you read a text, you read it through the lens of your own experience. Your understanding of the words on the page and their significance is informed by what you have come to know and value from living in a particular time and place. But the texts you read were all written in the past, sometimes in a radically different time and place. To read critically, you need to contextualize, to recognize the differences between your contemporary values and attitudes and those represented in the text.

Asking Questions about the Content

As students, you are accustomed to teachers asking you questions about your reading. These questions are designed to help you understand a reading and respond to it more fully, and often this technique works. When you need to understand and use new information though it is most beneficial if you write the questions, as you read the text for the first time. With this strategy, you can write questions any time, but in difficult academic readings, you will understand the material better and remember it longer if you write a question for every paragraph or brief section. Each question should focus on a main idea, not on illustrations or details, and each should be expressed in your own words, not just copied from parts of the paragraph.

Examining your Personal Responses

The reading that you do for this class might challenge your attitudes, your unconsciously held beliefs, or your positions on current issues. As you read a text for the first time, mark an X in the margin at each point where you fell a personal challenge to your attitudes, beliefs, or status. Make a brief note in the margin about what you feel or about what in the text created the challenge. Now look again at the places you marked in the text where you felt personally challenged. What patterns do you see?

Outlining and Summarizing

Outlining and summarizing are especially helpful strategies for understanding the content and structure of a reading selection. Whereas outlining revels the basic structure of the text, summarizing synopsizes a selection's main argument in brief. Outlining may be part of the annotating process, or it may be done separately (as it is in this class). The key to both outlining and summarizing is being able to distinguish between the main ideas and the supporting ideas and examples. The main ideas form the backbone, the strand that hold the various parts and pieces of the text together. Outlining the main ideas helps you to discover this structure. When you make an outline, don't use the text's exact words.

Summarizing begins with outlining, but instead of merely listing the main ideas, a summary recomposes them to form a new text. Whereas outlining depends on a close analysis of each paragraph, summarizing also requires creative synthesis. Putting ideas together again — in your own words and in a condensed form — shows how reading critically can lead to deeper understanding of any text.

Evaluating an Argument

All writers make assertions that want you to accept as true. As a critical reader, you should not accept anything on face value but to recognize every assertion as an argument that must be carefully evaluated. An argument has two essential parts: a claim and support. The claim asserts a conclusion

— an idea, an opinion, a judgment, or a point of view — that the writer wants you to accept. The support includes reasons (shared beliefs, assumptions, and values) and evidence (facts, examples, statistics, and authorities) that give readers the basis for accepting the conclusion. When you assess an argument, you are concerned with the process of reasoning as well as its truthfulness (these are not the same thing). At the most basic level, in order for an argument to be acceptable, the support must be appropriate to the claim and the statements must be consistent with one another.

Comparing and Contrasting Related Readings

Many of the authors we read are concerned with the same issues or questions, but approach how to discuss them in different ways. Fitting a text into an ongoing dialectic helps increase understanding of why an author approached a particular issue or question in the way he or she did.

Using Authentic Materials and Approaches

For students to develop communicative competence in reading, classroom and homework reading activities must resemble (or be) real-life reading tasks that involve meaningful communication. They must therefore be authentic in three ways.

1. *The reading material must be authentic:* It must be the kind of material that students will need and want to be able to read when traveling, studying abroad, or using the language in other contexts outside the classroom.

When selecting texts for student assignments, remember that the difficulty of a reading text is less a function of the language, and more a function of the conceptual difficulty and the task(s) that students are expected to complete. Simplifying a text by changing the language often removes natural redundancy and makes the organization somewhat difficult for students to predict. This actually makes a text more difficult to read than if the original were used.

Rather than simplifying a text by changing its language, make it more approachable by eliciting students' existing knowledge in pre-reading discussion, reviewing new vocabulary before reading, and asking students to perform tasks that are within their competence, such as skimming to get the main idea or scanning for specific information, before they begin intensive reading.

2. *The reading purpose must be authentic:* Students must be reading for reasons that make sense and have relevance to them. "Because the teacher assigned it" is not an authentic reason for reading a text.

   To identify relevant reading purposes, ask students how they plan to use the language they are learning and what topics they are interested in reading and learning about. Give them opportunities to choose their reading assignments, and encourage them to use the library, the Internet, and foreign language newsstands and bookstores to find other things they would like to read.

3. *The reading approach must be authentic*: Students should read the text in a way that matches the reading purpose, the type of text, and the way people normally

read. This means that reading aloud will take place only in situations where it would take place outside the classroom, such as reading for pleasure. The majority of students' reading should be done silently.

Reading Aloud in the Classroom

Students do not learn to read by reading aloud. A person who reads aloud and comprehends the meaning of the text is coordinating word recognition with comprehension and speaking and pronunciation ability in highly complex ways. Students whose language skills are limited are not able to process at this level, and end up having to drop one or more of the elements. Usually the dropped element is comprehension, and reading aloud becomes word calling: simply pronouncing a series of words without regard for the meaning they carry individually and together. Word calling is not productive for the student who is doing it, and it is boring for other students to listen to.

— There are two ways to use reading aloud productively in the language classroom. Read aloud to your students as they follow along silently. You have the ability to use inflection and tone to help them hear what the text is saying. Following along as you read will help students move from word-by-word reading to reading in phrases and thought units, as they do in their first language.

— Use the "read and look up" technique. With this technique, a student reads a phrase or sentence silently as many times as necessary, then looks up (away from the text) and tells you what the phrase or sentence says. This encourages students to read for ideas, rather than for word recognition.

Strategies for Developing Reading Skills

Language instructors are often frustrated by the fact that students do not automatically transfer the strategies they use when reading in their native language to reading in a language they are learning. Instead, they seem to think reading means starting at the beginning and going word by word, stopping to look up every unknown vocabulary item, until they reach the end. When they do this, students are relying exclusively on their linguistic knowledge, a bottom-up strategy. One of the most important functions of the language instructor, then, is to help students move past this idea and use top-down strategies as they do in their native language.

Effective language instructors show students how they can adjust their reading behavior to deal with a variety of situations, types of input, and reading purposes. They help students develop a set of reading strategies and match appropriate strategies to each reading situation.

Strategies that can help students read more quickly and effectively include :

— *Previewing*: reviewing titles, section headings, and photo captions to get a sense of the structure and content of a reading selection

— *Predicting*: using knowledge of the subject matter to make predictions about content and vocabulary and check comprehension; using knowledge of the text type and purpose to make predictions about discourse structure; using knowledge about the author to make predictions about writing style, vocabulary, and content

— *Skimming and scanning*: using a quick survey of the text to get the main idea, identify text structure, confirm or question predictions

— *Guessing from context*: using prior knowledge of the subject and the ideas in the text as clues to the meanings of unknown words, instead of stopping to look them up

— *Paraphrasing*: stopping at the end of a section to check comprehension by restating the information and ideas in the text

Instructors can help students learn when and how to use reading strategies in several ways.

— By modeling the strategies aloud, talking through the processes of previewing, predicting, skimming and scanning, and paraphrasing. This shows students how the strategies work and how much they can know about a text before they begin to read word by word.

— By allowing time in class for group and individual previewing and predicting activities as preparation for in-class or out-of-class reading. Allocating class time to these activities indicates their importance and value.

— By using cloze exercises to review vocabulary items. This helps students learn to guess meaning from context.

— By encouraging students to talk about what strategies they think will help them approach a reading assignment, and then talking after reading about what strategies they actually used. This helps students develop flexibility in their choice of strategies.

When language learners use reading strategies, they find that they can control the reading experience, and they gain confidence in their ability to read the language.

Reading to Learn

Reading is an essential part of language instruction at every level because it supports learning in multiple ways.

— Reading to learn the language: Reading material is language input. By giving students a variety of materials to read, instructors provide multiple opportunities for students to absorb vocabulary, grammar, sentence structure, and discourse structure as they occur in authentic contexts. Students thus gain a more complete picture of the ways in which the elements of the language work together to convey meaning.

— Reading for content information: Students' purpose for reading in their native language is often to obtain information about a subject they are studying, and this purpose can be useful in the language learning classroom as well. Reading for content information in the language classroom gives students both authentic reading material and an authentic purpose for reading.

— Reading for cultural knowledge and awareness: Reading everyday materials that are designed for native speakers can give students insight into the lifestyles and worldviews of the people whose language they are studying. When students have access to newspapers, magazines, and Web sites, they are exposed to culture in all its variety, and monolithic cultural stereotypes begin to break down.

When reading to learn, students need to follow four basic steps:

— Figure out the purpose for reading. Activate background knowledge of the topic in order to predict or anticipate content and identify appropriate reading strategies.

— Attend to the parts of the text that are relevant to the identified purpose and ignore the rest. This selectivity enables students to focus on specific items in the input and reduces the amount of information they have to hold in short-term memory.

— Select strategies that are appropriate to the reading task and use them flexibly and interactively. Students' comprehension improves and their confidence increases when they use top-down and bottom-up skills simultaneously to construct meaning.

— Check comprehension while reading and when the reading task is completed. Monitoring comprehension helps students detect inconsistencies and comprehension failures, helping them learn to use alternate strategies.

Developing Reading Activities

Developing reading activities involves more than identifying a text that is "at the right level," writing a set of comprehension questions for students to answer after reading, handing out the assignment and sending students away to do it. A fully-developed reading activity supports students as readers through prereading, while-reading, and post-reading activities.

As you design reading tasks, keep in mind that complete recall of all the information in a text is an unrealistic expectation even for native speakers. Reading activities that are meant to increase communicative competence should be success oriented and build up students' confidence in their reading ability.

Construct the Reading Activity around a Purpose that has Significance for the Students

Make sure students understand what the purpose for reading is: to get the main idea, obtain specific information, understand most or all of the message, enjoy a story, or decide whether or not to read more. Recognizing the purpose for reading will help students select appropriate reading strategies.

Define the Activity's Instructional Goal and the Appropriate Type of Response

In addition to the main purpose for reading, an activity can also have one or more instructional purposes, such as practicing or reviewing specific grammatical constructions, introducing new vocabulary, or familiarizing students with the typical structure of a certain type of text.

Check the Level of Difficulty of the Text

The factors listed below can help you judge the relative ease or difficulty of a reading text for a particular purpose and a particular group of students.

— How is the information organized? Does the story line, narrative, or instruction conform to familiar expectations? Texts in which the events are presented in natural chronological order, which have an informative title, and which present the information following an obvious organization (main ideas first, details and examples second) are easier to follow.

— How familiar are the students with the topic? Remember that misapplication of background knowledge due to cultural differences can create major comprehension difficulties.

— Does the text contain redundancy? At the lower levels of proficiency, listeners may find short, simple messages easier to process, but students with higher proficiency benefit from the natural redundancy of authentic language.

— Does the text offer visual support to aid in reading comprehension? Visual aids such as photographs, maps, and diagrams help students preview the content of the text, guess the meanings of unknown words, and check comprehension while reading.

Remember that the level of difficulty of a text is not the same as the level of difficulty of a reading task. Students who lack the vocabulary to identify all of the items on a menu can still determine whether the restaurant serves steak and whether they can afford to order one.

Use Pre-reading Activities to Prepare Students for Reading

The activities you use during pre-reading may serve as preparation in several ways. During pre-reading you may:

— Assess students' background knowledge of the topic and linguistic content of the text

— Give students the background knowledge necessary for comprehension of the text, or activate the existing knowledge that the students possess

— Clarify any cultural information which may be necessary to comprehend the passage

— Make students aware of the type of text they will be reading and the purpose(s) for reading

— Provide opportunities for group or collaborative work and for class discussion activities

Sample Pre-reading Activities

— Using the title, subtitles, and divisions within the text to predict content and organization or sequence of information

— Looking at pictures, maps, diagrams, or graphs and their captions

— Talking about the author's background, writing style, and usual topics

— Skimming to find the theme or main idea and eliciting related prior knowledge

— Reviewing vocabulary or grammatical structures

— Reading over the comprehension questions to focus attention on finding that information while reading

— Constructing semantic webs (a graphic arrangement of concepts or words showing how they are related)

— Doing guided practice with guessing meaning from context or checking comprehension while reading

Pre-reading activities are most important at lower levels of language proficiency and at earlier stages of reading instruction. As students become more proficient at using reading strategies, you will be able to reduce the amount of guided pre-reading and allow students to do these activities themselves.

Match While-reading Activities to the Purpose for Reading

In while-reading activities, students check their comprehension as they read. The purpose for reading determines the appropriate type and level of comprehension.

— When reading for specific information, students need to ask themselves, have I obtained the information I was looking for?

— When reading for pleasure, students need to ask themselves, Do I understand the story line/sequence of ideas well enough to enjoy reading this?

— When reading for thorough understanding (intensive reading), students need to ask themselves, Do I understand each main idea and how the author supports it? Does what I'm reading agree with my predictions, and, if not, how does it differ? To check comprehension in this situation, students may

— Stop at the end of each section to review and check their predictions, restate the main idea and summarize the section

— Use the comprehension questions as guides to the text, stopping to answer them as they read

Using Textbook Reading Activities

Many language textbooks emphasize product (answers to comprehension questions) over process (using reading skills and strategies to understand the text), providing little or no contextual information about the reading selections or their authors, and few if any pre-reading activities. Newer textbooks may provide pre-reading activities and reading strategy guidance, but their one-size-fits-all approach may or may not be appropriate for your students.

You can use the guidelines for developing reading activities given here as starting points for evaluating and adapting textbook reading activities. Use existing, or add your own, pre-reading activities and reading strategy practice as appropriate for your students. Don't make students do exercises simply because they are in the book; this destroys motivation.

Another problem with textbook reading selections is that they have been adapted to a predetermined reading level through adjustment of vocabulary, grammar, and sentence length. This makes them more immediately approachable, but it also means that they are less authentic and do not encourage students to apply the reading strategies they will need to use outside of class. When this is the case, use the textbook reading selection as a starting point to introduce a writer or topic, and then give students choices of more challenging authentic texts to read as a followup.

Role of Phonics in Teaching of Reading

A reputable body of research substantiates the positive effects of well-designed phonics instruction and provides guidance about the form that instruction should take. The following research conclusions guided the development of Houghton Mifflin's newly published program, Invitations to Literacy:

— Phonics is an essential part of a comprehensive approach to the teaching of reading.

- Phonics instruction needs to be explicit and direct; incidental and opportunistic approaches to developing phonics are less effective.
- Phonics instruction can and must be meaningful, lively, and engaging; phonics should not be equated with repetitious drill or the mindless completion of worksheets.
- In order for children to gain full use of phonics skills they need guidance in integrating them with other word identification skills and in strategically and fluently applying those skills.
- In order for children to gain full use of phonics skills they need many opportunities to apply them to functional and interesting reading and writing activities.
- While the development of phonics and other word identification skills is essential and necessary for skillful, mature reading, it is not sufficient; skillful mature reading must also build upon language, vocabulary, and concept development as well as a variety of thinking skills.

Based on the available research, Houghton Mifflin incorporated into Invitations to Literacy the following essential components of an effective program for development of word identification skills and reading fluency:

Phonological/Phonemic Awareness

In order to learn to read an alphabetical language like English, children must grasp what is called the alphabetic principle—that printed words are not an arbitrary sequence of letters to be memorized, but that letters represent a limited number of speech sounds that combine to form spoken words. Young children do not intuitively grasp this principle nor do they think of spoken words as having any dimension other than meaning. Phonological awareness refers to children's conscious awareness of the fact that spoken words are composed of identifiable units including syllables, rimes, and sounds (phonemes). It also refers to children's ability to manipulate (segment, blend, substitute) those sound units.

In the Kindergarten level of Invitations to Literacy children are taught concepts of rhyme and beginning sounds, the most fundamental phonological awareness skills. They also become proficient in blending and segmenting onsets (the initial consonant or consonants, e.g., the s in sit) and rimes (the remainder of a one syllable word, e.g., the -it in sit). In addition to building phonemic awareness, instruction in onsets and rimes prepares children to read words by analogy. (For example, a child who knows initial consonants and the rime -it in sit can likely read hit.)

In Grade 1, phonological and phonemic skills are extended and refined. As children encounter words they cannot read, they are taught to use their knowledge of letter sound associations and to blend the phonemes into meaningful, spoken words. Segmenting the sounds of the spoken words and representing them with letters are taught and practiced frequently as children grow in their spelling abilities.

Familiarity with Print

There are several dimensions of familiarity with print including:

— *Letter Names/Shapes:* Knowledge of letter names is highly associated with success in beginning reading. In Invitations to Literacy children learn to recognize letters accurately and quickly. Letter names are, in most cases, good clues to letter sound associations. Being able to form letters quickly is important for writing, which reinforces and extends phonological awareness, knowledge of letter/sound associations, and familiarity with the form of written and spoken words.

— *Concepts of Print:* Children become familiar with concepts of letter, word, sentence, and the relationships of printed and spoken words. They develop the understanding that there is a correspondence between the number of words printed and the number of words read, and they are taught to use this concept to track print.

— *High Frequency Vocabulary:* While phonics skills can be used to identify printed words, many frequently used words are not phonically regular; these words must be recognized accurately and quickly. In Invitations to Literacy children are taught these words and have frequent opportunities to practice them in reading for fluency and in their writing.

— *Systematic, Explicit Phonics:* Phonics instruction in Invitations to Literacy is systematic in that it introduces children to more simple, stable letter/sound relationships (e.g., regular consonants) and then introduces more complex and variable elements (e.g., vowels and vowel pairs). Many common letter patterns are highly regular and common (e.g., -it, -en, -og); they are introduced early. All essential phonic elements are taught.

Phonics instruction is explicit; children are directly and clearly taught about relationships between letters and sounds. They have many opportunities to practice and apply these learnings in a variety of ways, including manipulating letters to build words and applying phonics skills to decodable texts and to writing. Through phonics and spelling instruction children develop the ability to segment and blend phonemes and to sound out words by blending letter sounds from left to right.

— *Spelling:* In Invitations to Literacy spelling and phonics are integrally related. Phonics elements that are taught in a unit of instruction are reinforced in spelling instruction in the same unit. In spelling lessons, children learn to carefully process the letters in words from left to right and to segment and blend the sounds the letters represent.

— *Vocabulary*: Beyond the initial stages of learning to read, there is a very strong relationship between knowledge of word meanings and reading comprehension. Vocabulary instruction and learning to derive word meanings from context begin in kindergarten and continue throughout Invitations to Literacy.

— *Fluent Reading*: Decodable text is essential to provide opportunities for children to practice and apply phonic elements in the context of real reading. Invitations to Literacy includes many decodable books for practice with high frequency words and words that use previously taught phonic elements. In addition to a wide variety of reading materials that are part of the program, Invitations to Literacy provides carefully developed reading lists, frequent suggestions to teachers, and extensive communications with the home to encourage the wide independent reading that leads to fluency.

— *Writing*: Writing offers the opportunity to apply phonics and related spelling knowledge. In shared writing and other writing activities, children learn to think about the sounds in words they want to write and to use phonics skills to represent the sounds. As they proofread their writing, they apply spelling patterns and phonic elements they have been taught.

Assessing Reading Proficiency

Reading ability is very difficult to assess accurately. In the communicative competence model, a student's reading level is the level at which that student is able to use reading to accomplish communication goals. This means that assessment of reading ability needs to be correlated with purposes for reading.

Reading Aloud

A student's performance when reading aloud is not a reliable indicator of that student's reading ability. A student who is perfectly capable of understanding a given text when reading it silently may stumble when asked to combine comprehension with word recognition and speaking ability in the way that reading aloud requires.

In addition, reading aloud is a task that students will rarely, if ever, need to do outside of the classroom. As a method of assessment, therefore, it is not authentic: It does not test a student's ability to use reading to accomplish a purpose or goal.

However, reading aloud can help a teacher assess whether a student is "seeing" word endings and other grammatical features when reading. To use reading aloud for this purpose, adopt the "read and look up" approach: Ask the student to read a sentence silently one or more times, until comfortable with the content, then look up and tell you what it says. This procedure allows the student to process the text, and lets you see the results of that processing and know what elements, if any, the student is missing.

Comprehension Questions

Instructors often use comprehension questions to test whether students have understood what they have read. In order to test comprehension appropriately, these questions need to be coordinated with the purpose for reading. If the purpose is to find specific information, comprehension questions should focus on that information. If the purpose is to understand an opinion and the arguments that support it, comprehension questions should ask about those points.

In everyday reading situations, readers have a purpose for reading before they start. That is, they know what comprehension questions they are going to need to answer before they begin reading. To make reading assessment in the language classroom more like reading outside of the classroom, therefore, allow students to review the comprehension questions before they begin to read the test passage.

Finally, when the purpose for reading is enjoyment, comprehension questions are beside the point. As a more authentic form of assessment, have students talk or write about why they found the text enjoyable and interesting (or not).

Authentic Assessment

In order to provide authentic assessment of students' reading proficiency, a post-listening activity must reflect the real-life uses to which students might put information they have gained through reading.

— It must have a purpose other than assessment

— It must require students to demonstrate their level of reading comprehension by completing some task

To develop authentic assessment activities, consider the type of response that reading a particular selection would elicit in a non-classroom situation. For example, after reading a weather report, one might decide what to wear the next day; after reading a set of instructions, one might repeat them to someone else; after reading a short story, one might discuss the story line with friends.

Use this response type as a base for selecting appropriate post-reading tasks. You can then develop a checklist or rubric that will allow you to evaluate each student's comprehension of specific parts of the text.

Role of Parents in Improving Youngsters' Reading Skills

Approximately 20 to 30 percent of school-age children have difficulties learning to read. Many million youngsters do not have access to the wonders of books and other kinds of texts for learning and enjoyment. Almost as many girls as boys experience difficulties learning to read. Boys seem to be identified as reading disabled more readily because they tend to be more active and boisterous than their female agemates. While these estimates are alarming, they are on the conservative side.

Are there other consequences of not learning to read? Indeed there are. If you observe children with reading difficulties, many negative effects become apparent. During the early grades, their difficulties are quite embarrassing to them. This humiliation leads to a predictable decrease in motivation and self-esteem. Children are easily frustrated and ashamed of their difficulties once they notice that many of their classmates read so effortlessly. As the youngsters mature, many of them drop out of school and of the those who manage to graduate from high school less than two percent attend a four year college.

Skilled reading requires the integration of several skills and abilities. You cannot learn to read an alphabetic language like English, unless you understand that the words that you hear contain smaller sounds called "phonemes." Phonemes cannot actually be "heard" by the ear because when we speak the sounds in each syllable and word are folded into one sound to permit rapid communication. Thus, when speaking the word /cat/, the ear hears one sound, not three as in /c/ /a/ /t/. Many readers must be taught "phoneme awareness" if it does not come easily to them.

Understanding that spoken words are composed of phonemes is critical because in beginning reading, new words are decoded by linking the phonemes to the letter symbols. Once children learn how to apply sounds to letter symbols, they must practice the process to ensure that their reading becomes rapid and fluent. Reading requires phoneme awareness, phonics, reading fluency, and comprehension skills. Each of these skills are necessary and none are sufficient in their own right. They must be integrated and applied in text through consistent and frequent practice. Learning to read is not a natural process—it requires systematic and well informed instruction.

Most reading problems can be observed when the child attempts to read out loud. You will notice a labored approach to decoding or "sounding out" unknown or unfamiliar words. Reading is typically hesitant and characterized by frequent starts and stops. If asked about the meaning of what was just read, the individual frequently has little to say. Not because he or she isn't smart enough: in fact, many people with reading problems are very bright. Poor comprehension occurs because they take too long to read the words, leaving little energy for remembering and understanding what was read.

Individuals who are most at-risk for reading difficulties are those who enter school with limited exposure to oral language interactions and little prior understanding of concepts related to the sounds of our language, letter knowledge, print awareness, and general verbal skills. Children raised in poverty, with limited proficiency in English, speech and hearing impairments, or from homes where little reading takes place are especially at-risk for reading failure. However, there are a substantial number of children who have had substantial exposure to language, literacy interactions, and opportunities to learn to read who have significant difficulties acquiring reading skills. Whether the causes are environmental or genetic in nature, the reading problems occur due to deficits in phoneme awareness, phonics development, reading fluency, reading comprehension or, frequently, combinations of these.

Most children can learn to read if difficulties are detected in kindergarten and first grade and the appropriate early interventions are applied. Prevention and early intervention programs that teach phoneme awareness and phonics skills and develop reading contexts where children have an opportunity to practice skills are more beneficial than approaches that are less structured and direct. Help needs to be provided before nine years of age, after that time, children respond poorer to reading instruction.

The most important thing that parents can do is talk and read to their children. During the toddler and preschool years it is critical to provide children with many different language and reading experiences that are playful and fun, to include nursery rhymes and rhyming games to expose youngsters to the sounds of our language, lap-time reading, and bed-time reading. It is critical that young children observe their parents reading and learn why reading is so important in our lives. A major thing to remember is to make all of the language and literacy interactions in the home positive and enjoyable experiences

Parents are more concerned about their child's progress in reading than in any other subject taught in school, and rightfully so. In order for students to achieve in math, science, English, history, geography, and other subjects, reading skills must be developed to the point that most of them are automatic. Students cannot struggle with word recognition when they should be reading quickly for comprehension of a text.

Because reading is so important to success in school, parents can and should play a role in helping their children to become interested in reading and in encouraging their growth in reading skills. At the same time, parents and teachers need to work together. Many teachers are now sending home practical ideas for parents to use with their preschoolers. As a result, young children are developing some of the skills at home that will later help them in school.

Research shows that children learn about reading before they enter school. In fact, they learn in the best manner—

through observation. Young children, for example, see people around them reading newspapers, books, maps, and signs. Parents can do a lot to foster an understanding of print by talking with their preschoolers about signs in their environment and by letting their children know they enjoy reading themselves.

Many parents recognize the value and enjoyment of reading to their young children, but perhaps they are not clear about the specific skills that could be enhanced through the process. Most important, reading should be an enjoyable experience. Research reveals that when young children experience warm and close contacts with their parents when they are being read to, they develop more positive attitudes toward reading.

Run your index finger under the line of print. This procedure is simple and helps children begin to notice words and that words have meaning. They also gain an awareness of the conventions of reading (e.g., one reads from left to right and from the top of the page to the bottom; sentences are made up of words; and some sentences extend beyond a single line of print).

One of the greatest advantages of reading to preschoolers (or children of any age) is the opportunity for vocabulary development. Children learn the meaning of words through good literature; words take on rich meaning when used in an interesting story.

In the early elementary years, from first through third grades, children continue learning HOW to read. It is a complex process, difficult for some and easy for others. Care must be taken during these early years not to overemphasize the learning-to-read process. Reading for pleasure and information develops reading interests and offers children the opportunity to practice their reading skills in meaningful ways. Parents of elementary-age children should provide reading materials in the home that arouse curiosity or extend their child's natural interest in the world around them.

By encouraging and modeling leisure-time reading in the home, parents take the most important step in fostering their child's reading development.

Current research in reading reveals three important considerations for parents and teachers:

— Children who read, and read widely, become better readers.

— Reading and writing are complementary skills.

— Parents are important to children both as role models and as supporters of their efforts.

The following suggestions have been beneficial to many parents:

— Provide a good role model—read yourself and read often to your child.

— Provide varied reading material—some for reading enjoyment and some with information about hobbies and interests.

— Encourage activities that require reading—for example, cooking (reading a recipe), constructing a kite (reading directions), or identifying an interesting bird's nest or a shell collected at the beach (using a reference book).

— Establish a reading time, even if it is only 10 minutes a day.

— Write notes to your school-age child; encourage written responses.

— Ask your child to bring a library book home to read to a younger sibling.

— Establish one evening a week for reading (instead of television viewing).

— Encourage your child in all reading efforts.

6

Teaching Writing

A well-written piece can be described as incorporating elements of writing in such a way that a reader can experience the writer's intended meaning, understand the writer's premise, and accept or reject the writer's point of view.

Effective Writing:

- is focused on the topic and does not contain extraneous or loosely related information;
- has an organizational pattern that enables the reader to follow the flow of ideas because it contains a beginning, middle, and end and uses transitional devices;
- contains supporting ideas that are developed through the use of details, examples, vivid language, and mature word choice; and
- follows the conventions of standard written English (i.e., punctuation, capitalization, and spelling) and has variation in sentence structure.

The writing activities should be structured in ways that help students learn to produce cohesive and coherent discourse on their way to become self-sponsors of their own writings.

THE WRITING PROCESS

Writing is a complex process that allows writers to explore thoughts and ideas, and make them visible and concrete. Writing encourages thinking and learning for it motivates communication and makes thought available for reflection. When thought is written down, ideas can be examined, reconsidered, added to, rearranged, and changed.

Writing is most likely to encourage thinking and learning when students view writing as a process. By recognizing that writing is a recursive process, and that every writer uses the process in a different way, students experience less pressure to "get it right the first time" and are more willing to experiment, explore, revise, and edit. Yet, novice writers need to practice "writing" or exercises that involve copying or reproduction of learned material in order to learn the conventions of spelling, punctuation, grammatical agreement, and the like. Furthermore, students need to "write in the language" through engaging in a variety of grammar practice activities of controlled nature. Finally, they need to begin to write within a framework "flexibility measures" that include : transformation exercises, sentence combining, expansion, embellishments, idea frames, and similar activities).

Obviously, not all students of the same age or grade level write in the same way; students pass through several developmental writing stages:

Stage 1

Novice Writer (unskilled, unaware, teacher-dependent writer)

— has little, if any, individual style

— has little awareness of writing process

— has undeveloped skills and techniques

— seeks approval from teacher

— is reluctant to revise any writing

— believes good writing comes easily

Stage 2

Transitional Writer (transitional, self-involved, self-delineating writer)

— needs support and coaching in order to develop

— learns from modeled behaviors

— is developing a degree of comfort with the craft

— is anxious to stand alone, yet is uncomfortable with peer collaboration

— is developing an awareness of personal needs, interests, and preoccupations

Stage 3

Willing Writer (peer-involved, willing writer)

— is able to collaborate well with others

— requires external feedback to shape progress

— is able to profit from criticism

— is developing objectivity concerning work

— enjoys practicing craft

— is developing a sensitivity to audience

Stage 4

Independent Writer (independent, autonomous writer)

— makes highly objective self-assessments

— has developed a sophisticated personal style

— has developed a writer's voice

— takes risks and experiments

— is self-motivating and self-aware as a writer

— is a craftsperson

Approaches to Teaching Writing

There are several approaches to teaching writing that are presented by as follows:

The Controlled-to-Free Approach

In the 1950s and early 1960, the audio-lingual method dominated second-language learning This method emphasized speech and writing served to achieve mastery of grammatical and syntactic forms. Hence teachers developed and used techniques to enable student to achieve this mastery.

The controlled-to-free approach in is sequential: students are first given sentence exercises, then paragraphs to copy or manipulate grammatically by changing questions to statements, present to past, or plural to singular. They might also change words to clauses or combine sentences. With these controlled compositions, it is relatively easy to for students write and yet avoid errors, which makes error correction easy. Students are allowed to try some free composition after they have reached an intermediate level of proficiency. As such, this approach stress on grammar, syntax, and mechanics. It emphasizes accuracy rather than fluency or originality.

The Free-Writing Approach

This approach stresses writing quantity rather than quality. Teachers who use this approach assign vast amounts of free writing on given topics with only minimal correction. The emphasis in this approach is on content and fluency rather than on accuracy and form. Once ideas are down on the page, grammatical accuracy and organization follow. Thus, teachers may begin their classes by asking students to write freely on any topic without worrying about grammar and spelling for five or ten minutes.

The teachers does not correct these pieces of free writing. They simply read them and may comment on the ideas the writer expressed. Alternatively, some students may volunteer to read their own writing aloud to the class. Concern for "audience" and "content" are seen as important in this approach.

The Paragraph-Pattern Approach

Instead of accuracy of grammar or fluency of content, the Paragraph-Pattern-Approach stresses on organization. Students copy paragraphs and imitate model passages. They put scrambled sentences into paragraph order. They identify general and specific statements and choose to invent an appropriate topic sentence or insert or delete sentences. This approach is based on the principle that in different cultures people construct and organize communication with each other in different ways.

The Grammar-Syntax-Organization Approach

This approach stresses on simultaneous work on more than one composition feature. Teachers who follow this approach maintain that writing can not be seen as composed of separate skills which are learned sequentially. Therefore, student should be trained to pay attention to organization while they also work on the necessary grammar and syntax. This approach links the purpose of writing to the forms that are needed to convey message.

The Communicative Approach

This approach stresses the purpose of writing and the audience for it. Student writers are encouraged to behave like writers in real life and ask themselves the crucial questions about purpose and audience:

— Why am I writing this?

— Who will read it?

Traditionally, the teacher alone has been the audience for student writing. But some feel that writers do their best when writing is truly a communicative act, with a writer writing for a real reader. As such, the readership may be extended to classmate and pen pals.

The Process Approach

Recently, the teaching of writing has moved away from a concentration on written product to an emphasis on the process of writing. Thus, writers ask themselves:

— How do I write this?

— How do I get started?

In this approach, students are trained to generate ideas for writing, think of the purpose and audience, write multiple drafts in order to present written products that communicate their own ideas. Teachers who use this approach give students time to tray ideas and feedback on the content of what they write in their drafts. As such, writing becomes a process of discovery for the students as they discover new ideas and new language forms to express them.

Furthermore, learning to write is seen as a developmental process that helps students to write as professional authors do, choosing their own topics and genres, and writing from their own experiences or observations. A writing process approach requires that teachers give students greater responsibility for, and ownership of, their own learning. Students make decisions about genre and choice of topics, and collaborate as they write.

During the writing process, students engage in pre-writing, planning, drafting, and post-writing activities. However, as the writing process is recursive in nature, they do not necessarily engage in these activities in that order.

Model Activities

Activity 1: Simple Description with Visuals.

Have students examine a picture and ask them to name the objects in it. Then ask students to write a paragraph to describe the picture. The procedure for the activity may be as follows:

Provide the class with a picture of a room such as the one below. Ask students to label the objects in the picture and have them write a paragraph to describe the picture. Provide students with expressions and language structure if needed such as: "In the classroom there is " and have students complete the paragraph.

Activity 2: Completing a Description Paragraph.

Have students examine a picture and complete a description paragraph. The procedure for this activity may be as follows:

— Examine the picture in Activity 1 and complete the following paragraph:

> Mary lives in a very nice room. In her room, there is a ——, ———, and a ———. There are also several———. There are no ———, but Mary does have some ———. She wants to get a ——— for her wall and a ——— for the desk this afternoon when she goes shopping.

Activity 3: Completing a Description Paragraph

Give students a picture and have them complete a description by supplying the prepositions and expressions required by the context. The procedure for this activity may be as follows:

— Have students examine the picture in Activity 1 and complete the following paragraph:

> This is a picture of Mary's room. Her bed is ——— the window. ——— the bed and the window is a small chest of drawers. There is a bookcase ——— her bed on the ———. She has a radio that is ——— the book case, and she puts her books ——— the book case ——— three shelves. ——— the room. She has a very nice desk where she prepares her work for school.

Activity 4: Writing a Description from Questions.

Have students examine a picture and use a set of questions as a guide to write a short description of the picture. The procedure for this activity may be as follows:

— Examine the picture in Activity 1 and write a description of it, using the questions below as guide lines.

Questions :

1. Does Mary have a nice room?
2. What kind of things does she have in the room?
3. What do you like in Mary's room?
4. Do you have a room like Mary's room? Describe your room in a few sentences.

Activity 5: Slash Sentences

Give students a set of sentence cues and have them write a short narrative paragraph. The procedure for this activity may be as follows:

— Make comlete sentences according to the model.

Model: The Smiths / Summer / in the country/ spend

The Smiths spend Summer in the country.

1. all / family / In the morning / to get up / arround / 8'oclock.
2. Mr. Smith / the kitchen / coffee / to prepare / to go down strairs.
3. his / wife / then / breakfast / to go outside / in / the garden.

Activity 6: Sentence Combining

Give students a set of propositions and have them combine them into complete sentences. The procedure for this activity may be as follows:

a) Provide students with set of propositions such as the ones below:

1. The man is tall.
2. The man has dark hair.
3. The man is standing by the door.
4. The man looks suspicious

b) Have students combine the propositions in one sentence.

Activity 7: Composition based on oral interview.

Have students interview a partner and a composition telling what they learned about the person they interviewed. The procedure for this activity may be as follows:

a) Have students interview a partner a certain topics and have then write a composition to tell what they had learned about this partner sample topics:

1. Talk about yourself and your family (i.e., where are you from, where your family lives, your hobbies, etc...).
2. Talk about what you like and dislike about your school.
3. Describe a memorable event.
4. Describe your goals and future plans.
5. Describe a recent vacation.

Process Writing Activities

The following process writing activities can be used in cycle I & II of Basic Education.

Pre-writing: A Place to Start

Pre-writing, the first stage in the writing process, begins long before the writer puts thoughts into writing. The experiences, observations, and interactions that students have prior to entering the classroom have an impact upon what they will write and how they will write it. Within the classroom, pre-writing prompts and activities can be integrated into the writing process as scaffolds by teachers to help students generate ideas for their writing and to practice the thinking skills inherent in the activity.

To initiate thinking and generate possible writing topics, it is important for students to explore ideas for writing topics using a variety of pre-writing strategies, such as the following:

— Brainstorming

— Constructing thought webs and graphic organizers

— Interviewing a person knowledgeable about the topic

— Engaging in peer or teacher-student discussions and conferences

— Listening to music

— Reading about and researching the topic

— Free writing or timed free writing about the topic

— Viewing media such as pictures, movies, and television

— Listing and categorizing information

— Reflecting upon personal experience

— Examining writing models
— Responding to literature
— Role playing and other drama techniques
— Asking the 5 Ws—who, what, where, when and why.

To explore topics about which to write, the teacher may post suggestions on the bulletin board for student reference. He/she may invite students to add their own pre-writing strategies to ideas such as the following:

1. Brainstorming about people, places, and feelings

Write down or tell a partner the names of people you could describe, then quickly and briefly describe each one. Name several places you have visited and list descriptive words for each place. List and describe some memorable feelings you have had, and explain the situation in which they occurred.

2. Talking and listening in pairs or groups

Take turns telling about an interesting person, thing, incident, or object. Encourage the listeners to ask questions and add ideas. Record possible writing topics or ideas as they arise during the discussion.

3. Looking at art

Study paintings, photographs, drawings, or sculpture in magazines or art books. It may even be useful to take a trip to a local museum or art gallery. Jot down notes and questions about the artwork, the artist and the subject, and any topic ideas that come to mind during the observation. It may help to talk over your information and ideas with a partner or small group. Explain to a partner the stories in the art works.

4. Listening to music

Listen to music you like best or a variety of new and unfamiliar music. Listen to tape recordings or to the radio, closing your eyes and letting the music paint pictures in your mind. Record these images as you listen, or turn off the music and quickly record your ideas. It may be helpful to tell the story you have imagined to a partner or group.

5. Role playing

Pretend to be any character, ask peers to act as other characters, and dramatize an event or incident, and what happened as a result of that incident or event.

6. Observing with all senses

Be aware of all that is happening around you, in the classroom, at home, in restaurants, in malls, and wherever you go. Listen closely to conversations of the people you observe, and try to capture the details of their manners and dress. Observe for issues, problems, or achievements in your community. Jot down ideas and notes as you observe them or as soon as possible after your observations.

7. Listing ideas and information

List such things as the activities that interest you, the sports you play, the clubs that you belong to, and the community and world issues that you know about from the media.

8. Reading

Read such things as nonfiction books, novels, magazines, stories, newspapers, and poems. Jot down ideas that occur to you as you read and list questions you might investigate further. Keep track of interesting vocabulary, story plots, and characters.

9. Newspaper searches

Read the stories and captions that catch your interest. Jot down ideas for writing a newspaper article or ideas that can be developed into other kinds of writing.

10. Author visits

As the authors share their writing and discuss the craft of writing, students gain further understanding of the writing process and possibly get ideas for their own writing.

Pre-writing prompts or activities planned by the teacher can serve as writing scaffolds for inexperienced writers who have difficulty accessing their own feelings, ideas, experiences, and knowledge. Teacher-planned pre-writing activities, such as the samples that follow, give students a place to start and make them become aware of places from which to get ideas in the future. Students who have a place to start with will be more motivated to continue developing their ideas and their own writing voices.

Sample Pre-writing Activity 1

Time allotment (5-10 minutes)

— Give each student any book or magazine to use (e.g., Readers' Digest, anthologies). The teacher should have a selection also, in order to model the process.

— Have students open their books or magazines at any page and choose a word at random—the first word that jumps off the page at them—and record this as Word 1; close the book.

— Continue this until each student has four words recorded. Students then focus for about one minute on each word separately, and list all their thoughts, ideas and associations that the word generates. Students then begin to make connections among the four words and their lists of personal associations by writing phrases, sentences, and ideas that demonstrate a relationship among the words. Students now have had a writing warm-up and may continue developing the ideas generated or bank these ideas for another day's writing.

Sample Pre-writing Activity 2

Time allotment (5-12 minutes)

— Teachers may request that students bring pictures of people, or the teacher may supply them (photographs or pictures clipped from magazines). Each picture should show several people in sufficient detail to reveal size, facial expression, dress, and other facets of character.

Quickly walk the students through this activity, question by question, so they record the first thoughts and reactions that the pictures generate, rather than dwelling too long on one question. The teacher should ask students to examine their pictures closely, and explain that they will need to use their imagination for the activity. Some questions the teacher might ask are:

— Who is the main character in the picture?

— What is an appropriate name for this character?

— How old is this character?

— What emotions is this character showing in the picture? Describe the evidence that you have for this (e.g., facial expression, gestures).

— What kind of work might the character do for a living? Give reasons to support your decision.

— What might the person be thinking or saying? What makes you imagine this?

— What other characteristics are revealed by the character's dress and stance?

— What might have happened before the picture was taken? What might happen next?

— How are the other characters in the picture related to the main character? What evidence makes you think so?

— What is the attitude of the main character to the other characters? What is the attitude of the other characters to the main character? What are some possible reasons for these attitudes?

— What might it be like to be the main character or one of the other characters?

Instruct students to record ideas briefly, using phrases and words rather than sentences. Students then may take the opportunity to develop their ideas further, or save their notes and ideas for use at a later date.

Sample Pre-writing Activity 3

Time allotment (5-8 minutes)

— Prepare the students for free writing by explaining that they should write whatever thoughts enter their head from the moment that the teacher says "go" to the moment he/she says "stop", even if it means writing and rewriting, I don't know what to write. I don't know what to write. When the pen or pencil hits the paper it does not stop for pauses, erasures, or corrections. Eventually, most students begin to focus and the writing flows. Students then have the opportunity to develop these pre-writing ideas further or save them for another day.

Organizing for Drafting

After students have generated some ideas, they must decide what they will say about their chosen topic. Students develop an initial plan for the product they will compose. As they do so, they must consider the purpose, audience, point of view, and format because these elements have implications for both the planning and the drafting of the written product.

To develop an initial plan for drafting, students organize the information they have generated during pre-writing by using such structures as outlines, story frames, maps, diagrams, charts, and concept webs.

To consider purpose, students write to express ideas, feelings, emotions, and opinions, and they must ask themselves, "What is my purpose for writing this piece?" Some purposes for students' writings are:

1. to express personal feelings or viewpoints
2. to imagine "What if ...?"
3. to narrate
4. to entertain and/or amuse
5. to describe

6. to inform or explain
7. to persuade or convince
8. to request
9. to inquire or question
10. to explore and experiment with ideas and formats
11. to clarify thinking.

To consider audience, students must consider who they are writing for and students must ask themselves, "Who is my intended audience?" Some possible audiences are:

1. *familiar, known audiences*: self, friends, peers, family, teachers
2. *extended, known audiences*: community, student body, local media
3. *extended, unknown audiences*: wider range of media and other publications

To consider point of view, students must determine from which point of view their ideas or information will be expressed, so they need to ask themselves, "Who is telling this story/describing the events?" Some points of view for students' consideration are:

1. physical point of view: where is the narrator in relation to the action?
2. objective and subjective point of view: what emotional involvement does the narrator have in relation to the situation?
3. personal point of view: who is the narrator of the story? (The narrator may take a first person, third person, or an all-knowing omniscient point of view.)

To decide what information will be gathered and how it will most effectively be gathered, students who decide that they need to conduct interviews or go on field trips to gather information will need to brainstorm and construct a list of questions. Students who require library research will need to decide the types of resources and references to consult.

To consider format, students will use audience and purpose to determine format and genre. They will have the opportunity to write in a variety of narrative, descriptive, expository, and poetic formats. Their writings may include formats and genres such as: advertisement, advice column, autobiography/biography, comic strip, letter of complaint/request/inquiry, diary/journal, readers theater/role play/monologue, book review, report, fable/fairy tale, greeting card, game rules, directions, interview, news story, poem/song, anecdote/personal experience story, sports column, short story, etc.

Drafting: A Time to Indulge

At this point in the process, the emphasis is on content and meaning rather than on mechanics and conventions. This is the time for writers to get down their ideas and thoughts, composing rough drafts based upon pre-writing and planning activities and considerations. As they compose, writers begin to determine what to include and exclude, and make initial decisions about how these ideas will be organized. During the drafting stage of the writing process, meaning begins to evolve.

— To produce a first, rough draft, students record their ideas rapidly in order to capture the essence of what they have to say. They do not have to make any attempt to revise or edit at this point. They focus on talking to the reader and begin to develop a personal style as their voices emerge.

— To write subsequent drafts, students often accomplish their work by crossing out, adding, and rearranging ideas directly on the page. The students' redrafting does not necessarily require an entire rewrite at this time.

— To reflect upon their own writing, students can conference with self, peers and the teacher. Through conferencing, students can get constructive feedback and support that may help them to shape their writings. A set of questions or a checklist can be used to assist writers and conference partners as they strive to help the writer make meaning clear.

Sample 1: Self-Conference Checklist

As you write ... Ask yourself some of these questions:

— How do I feel about what I've written so far?

— What is good that I can enhance?

— Is there anything about it that concerns me, does not fit, or seems wrong?

— What am I discovering as I write this piece?

— What surprises me? Where is it leading?

— What is my purpose?

— What is the one most important thing that I am trying to convey?

— How can I build this idea? Are there places that I wander away from my key idea?

— Who is my audience?

Sample 2: Teacher-Student Checklist

During the teacher-student conference the teacher may as questions such as

— What is the part that you like best?

— Does it say what you want it to say?

— What do you mean by...?

— Where/when does your story take place?

— Are you satisfied with the beginning/ending? Why or why not?

— Does this sentence/word/phrase make sense to you?

— What reaction do you want your reader to have?

— How do you see your ideas being rearranged or changed? Why?

Sample 3: Steps For A Peer Writing Conference

When peers are conferencing

1. The writer decides how the written work will be shared. Will it be:

   — read silently by the conference partner(s)?

   — read aloud by the writer?

   — read aloud by the conference partner(s)?

   — a combination of the above?

2. The writer identifies what aspects of the written work will be the focus of the conference (e.g., the beginning paragraph, figurative language).

3. The conference partner states at least:

— one thing he/she considers that the writer has done well

— one thing he/she especially likes

— one suggestion which addresses the focus of the conference as identified by the writer. (It is useful to have students complete a written conference sheet to guide their responses, especially when the process is new to them.)

4. The writer retains the right to the written work and is responsible for making the final decision about any changes.

— To revise the draft for content and clarity of meaning, students will reorganize and sequence relevant ideas, and add or delete details as they strive to make their meaning clear. Revisions can take place to words, sentences, paragraphs, or the whole piece (e.g., the writer may decide that the ideas would have more impact as poetry instead of prose).

— To edit the draft for mechanical and conventional concerns that detract from and obscure meaning, students will proofread for accuracy and correctness in spelling, punctuation, capitalization, grammar, and usage. Peer editing and editing partnerships or groups can be established to assist students who are at this stage in the process. The use of self and peer-editing checklists can be useful tools.

— To focus purpose, audience, and point of view, and confirm appropriateness of format, students have to reconsider and confirm the use of the variables, which were pondered during the planning stage.

Some suggestions for scaffolds at the drafting stage include the following:

— Post the major stages of a writing process (pre-writing, planning, drafting, post-writing) and brief information about each so that students can determine where they are at any time in the process.

— Help students develop criteria or tips for writing a particular genre or format (e.g., haiku, short story, letter), then post these on a bulletin board or have students record them in their notebooks for reference as they write.

— Set up a section of the classroom as a writing reference area and make available language resources such as dictionaries, thesauri, and grammar and usage texts. Encourage students to use these as needed individually or with peers and the teacher.

— Encourage students to use word-processing programs. This may be done in co-operation with teachers of Computer Science, Information Processing, or other areas of study where computers are used.

POST-WRITING

When students have an authentic audience and purpose, they want to rework their written drafts, polishing them for presentation or publication. Going public means taking a huge risk; the student's self-esteem is on the line, so the decision about how and with whom to share their writing must be up to the student writer. Teachers may encourage students to share certain pieces or determine the number of pieces that students are required to share or publish within a set time period, but ultimately the decision about which pieces to share, and with whom, should be left up to the writer.

To prepare a final, polished draft, students may write in legible handwriting or use a word-processing program to prepare a polished written work. Then their writings go to public through

1. Sharing
2. Publishing
3. Using a portfolio

Sharing

Students may share their written work. Sharing is a useful post- writing activity since it provides students with an immediate audience. Some examples of sharing students' writings include

1. The author's chair, which provides opportunity for students to share their writing aloud with the whole class;
2. Sharing in small groups or with a partner; and
3. Using bulletin board space assigned to a specific genre or to a class of students.

At times, students should be provided with opportunities to decide if they wish to share their written work, and whether they will share in pairs, in small groups, or with the whole class.

Publishing

Students may choose to publish their writing. Some examples of publishing formats include:

— Class booklets

— School or local newspapers

— Yearbook

— Writing contests

— Magazines

Using a portfolio

To decide if the written work will be placed in the student's assessment portfolio, teachers can negotiate with students to generate guidelines about the number and variety of pieces that they are required to place in their portfolio for assessment and evaluation purposes. Contracts may be useful to address individual student needs and abilities. Students should be involved in making choices about which of their written pieces will become part of their portfolios.

Some suggestions for post-writing scaffolds include the following:

— Discuss or develop with students the criteria for polished pieces. Post these or provide them as handouts for students to refer to as needed.

— Provide opportunities for students to use computer word-processing programs to create final drafts.

— Have students share their final compositions with classmates or with others in the community, such as younger children or elderly people.

— Post or publish students' work in the classroom and provide opportunities, when appropriate, for students to submit to publishers outside the classroom.

Mini-lessons

At some point during most writing classes, in a 5-10 minute mini-lesson (length depends upon the procedure, concept, skill, or convention to be taught), the teacher provides students with information necessary for their writing. Mini-lessons about language usage and conventions such as spelling, sentence structure, and punctuation are necessary; however, they should emerge from the students' writing or the curriculum objectives, rather than being arbitrarily determined by the teacher. It is important to allow time for students to practice concepts introduced in mini-lessons within the context of their own writing.

The decision about what to teach in a mini-lesson depends upon the selected objectives as well as upon the students' needs and interests. The following lists provide examples of topics that may require mini-lessons.

Writing Process Procedures

1. pre-writing activities
2. writing rough drafts
3. self-reflection
4. participating in writing groups
5. peer and teacher conferences
6. writing folders and assessment portfolios
7. revising and editing final drafts
8. sharing and publishing.

Literary Elements and Devices

1. plot
2. characters
3. main idea/theme
4. setting
5. narrative hook
6. point of view
7. flashbacks
8. foreshadowing
9. comparisons (e.g., analogies, metaphors, similes)
10. personification
11. alliteration
12. rhyme and repetition.

Language Conventions and Mechanics

1. writing sentences
2. varying sentence structure (adding, deleting, substituting, moving, and combining)
3. writing opening and concluding paragraphs
4. writing descriptive paragraphs
5. punctuating items in a series
6. using the apostrophe
7. choosing titles
8. punctuating dialogue
9. selecting appropriate words (e.g., to show fear, suspense, bravery, or other characteristics).

Writing Formats and Genre

1. friendly or business letter
2. news article
3. short story
4. haiku poetry
5. personal experience narrative
6. science fiction.

Some mini-lessons may be planned for the whole class because the teacher has determined the need for students to have specific information that supports their learning or the unit of study. Other mini-lessons may be provided to individuals or small groups as the need arises. If the concept to be taught is complex, the teacher should provide instruction in steps, allowing students the opportunity to practise each step before putting them all together.

Teachers should keep records (e.g., lesson plan sheets, anecdotal notes, checklists) of mini-lesson topics and to whom they were presented. Students may also be required to keep records of mini-lessons received (e.g., handouts, notes, checklists), for future reference.

Supporting and Managing the Writing Process

To support and manage a writing process workshop, teachers should take time to ensure that students understand how the classroom structure and instructional activities work together. It is important to create an atmosphere that allows and encourages students to feel safe taking risks in order to develop a community of writers who support each other and share with each other (the teacher is a part of this community).

The teacher should be sure that:

— desks are arranged in clusters or tables are used to accommodate four to six students.

— resources which will assist students as they write (e.g., dictionaries, language study texts, literature as models, and samples of student writing) are provided on a specified shelf.

— the writing process information is displayed on bulletin boards.

— the areas designated for specific activities (e.g., peer conferences, writing and publishing tasks) are set in the classroom.

Of course, the teacher plays an interactive role and builds scaffolds as needed. He/she should model the various writing formats and conventions of the writing process, and provide the needed help as each student is writing. As a member of the community of writers, the teacher also writes and shares his/her writing with the students. For instance, while the students are engaged in pre-writing, the teacher may do her/his writing on a chart for the students to observe. This models the process, as well as the specific format or conventions being used.

7

Improving Teaching Skills

IMPROVING LECTURING SKILLS

Most teachers lecture. Even those who embrace a modern view of participatory learning still turn to the lecture from time to time. As a teaching method, the lecture has been used for hundreds of years. Certainly, today, no student can acquire an advanced degree without listening to dozens of professors lecture. As perhaps with other teaching methods, the lecture gets a mixed review.

Although most of us have been inspired by brilliant lecturers, all of us have been bored, confused, and anesthetized by poor lecturers. We have vivid memories of the psychology teacher who read from his scripted notes without once looking up for an entire semester, the geography instructor who spoke to her maps, and the mathematics teacher who spoke so softly and obliquely that he could neither be heard nor understood. It is little wonder that we sometimes worry about our own lecturing practices, hoping that we will escape the traps that other well-intentioned teachers have fallen into.

Lecturing is essentially a form of public communication. We can borrow, then, from the public speaking literature to learn more about how to improve our lecturing skills. The ability to lecture well, like speaking well, is an acquired skill. However, unlike public speakers, as lecturers we have multiple opportunities to communicate with the same "audience." Thus, we can assess our mistakes, think analytically about our actions, and take steps to improve while teaching the same group of students. We may lecture as many as forty or more times to the same class. Improvement, then, is possible within the same semester as well as over several semesters or years.

As with any teaching method, the choice to lecture should be a strategic one. Lecturing is not the only way to teach, but it can be very effective if it is used with appropriate goals in mind. What are some objectives we might hope to achieve by lecturing? Among them are:

— Exercising/gaining control of the class

— Highlighting major ideas

— Setting the stage for forthcoming activities

— Showing one's own interest and enthusiasm for the subject

— Providing a role model of good public communication skills.

— Some brief elaboration may clarify.

Exercising/Gaining Control of the Class

Communication research clearly reveals that those who talk the most (in terms of frequency and duration) exert the most control over the rhetorical environment. The classroom is no exception. The teacher who chooses to lecture is asking students to listen. She is also setting the agenda, choosing the pacing and emphasis, and deciding the order in which concepts will be introduced. In addition, she sets the "rules" for interaction. Will she allow interrupting questions during the lecture? Will she save time after the lecture to address student concerns? The lecture, then, serves as a method of control over interaction patterns, organization, and substance.

Highlighting Major Ideas

Students are exposed to large quantities of information over the course of a semester. Sometimes, they find it difficult to distinguish major themes, ideas, or concepts from those of less importance. They may also find some of the material they encounter to be difficult or confusing. Through a lecture, the instructor can emphasize those concepts that are really valuable, help students put their knowledge in perspective, and through example and explanation, clarify confusions.

Although the number of major points stressed will vary with the length of the class and the sophistication of the student, generally students can absorb about three to five major ideas during a typical classroom lecture, with seven as an absolute maximum. Ideally, these major ideas should be broadly conceptual, presenting stimulating perspectives or idea scaffolds, upon which students can "hang" facts and attach their own insights and experiences.

Setting the Stage for Forthcoming Activities

In nearly every class, we ask students to perform many tasks. We may ask them to read a novel intelligently, prepare a persuasive speech, solve a set of math problems, observe a dramatic presentation, or pass a difficult examination. In some instances, we use these tasks to assess their knowledge and achievement. In other cases, we view the task as an opportunity for students to learn. Whatever our purposes, we want our students to understand the nature and purpose of the assigned task, to have a clear sense of our expectations, and to be well equipped to successfully grapple with the material.

One method of preparing students for their out-of-class learning is to set the stage with a lecture. If students were to watch a videotape of Mario Cuomo's speech to the 1984 Democratic convention, for instance, the instructor might lecture about the rhetorical environment in which the speech was delivered, highlighting Cuomo's background, his relationship to other candidates, and his likely role in the future of the Democratic Party. After listening to this kind of lecture, students should be reasonably well prepared to understand and learn from the speech.

Showing Your Enthusiasm for the Subject

It is probably safe to say that students do not always come to our classes with a high level of intrinsic interest in the subject. If the class is required (e.g., finite math, microeconomics, public speaking, freshman composition, accounting), students may view it as little more than a potential impediment to their career or professional school goals, as something to be endured, or overcome. This attitude stands in sharp contrast to our own. As teachers, we have devoted our intellectual lives to exploring our disciplines as subjects of great interest and intrinsic worth. When we lecture, through the way we speak, we have the opportunity to show our students how we feel about the subject.

If we speak with enthusiasm and energy, our students may eventually grow to better appreciate, and even enjoy, the subject. As Emerson once wrote, "the lecturer aims not to drill but to . . . set the hearts of youth aflame." However dramatic Emerson's statement, most of us can think of teachers with whom we studied who, through their love and enthusiasm, so influenced us that we were inspired to pursue our present disciplines. Like them, we, too, can teach with inspiration and conviction.

Providing a Public Speaking Role Model

Nearly every critique of higher education in America published during the past five years has bemoaned students' lack of oral and written communication skills. Every college graduate should be able to communicate effectively, to speak articulately and in an organized manner, to show a concern for clarity and conciseness, and to be able to support her views with evidence and sound reasoning. One way of attempting to improve students' oral communication skills is to ask every student to take a course in public speaking.

Another way is to expose students on a daily basis to good communication role models. The more we demonstrate through our lectures the sorts of qualities alluded to above, the more likely we are to have a positive impact on the way our students communicate. If we cannot establish eye contact with our students, if we ramble in a disorganized fashion, if we are unable to support our assertions with evidence, we will be hard pressed to expect better things of our students.

Developing Skills in Teaching and Learning Communication

Good communication is at the heart of best practice in social work. Indeed, social work was one of the first professions to recognise the importance of communications skills and how these skills link to effective practice. It is through our capacity to communicate that we relate and convey our respect and concern for others. Communication skills are also essential to the task of assessment and later decision making, not only for social workers but also for other professionals, particularly those working in the field of health and social care.

The importance of communication skills can also be seen in government policy, and the emphasis being placed on the role of service users and carers in relation to the new social work degree, and patients (consumers) in relation to health research, policy and practice. For all professions, the failure to communicate effectively can lead to serious - and sometimes tragic -consequences.

Theoretical Frameworks Underpinning Learning and Teaching of Communication Skills

A search of electronic databases was conducted by the Centre for Reviews and Dissemination (CRD) at the University of York using search terms agreed by the Working Group. This generated a vast literature of 8,023 records, mostly relating to communication skills for health professionals. Only records relating to the learning and teaching of communication skills for social care professionals were included in the review, with additional material identified by hand searching key journals and from group members' personal libraries.

From data identified in the York electronic database literature search, only 16 papers were identified as being relevant in their coverage of the theoretical frameworks informing the learning and teaching of communication skills in social work education - and many of these papers were quite dated. In some papers, the theoretical coverage tends to be implicit or, if explicit, tends to lack sufficient depth and critical analysis. There may be two reasons for this limited coverage of theory.

First, it may suggest that some authors do not consider it necessary to provide a detailed theoretical exploration, perhaps because it is assumed that most readers will know and understand the theoretical assumptions that underpin their work. This assumption may be correct for social work academics but one that calls for caution in relation to social work students and practitioners.

Second, it may suggest that some authors believe that an exploration of theory is not necessary in relation to skills learning and teaching. Whatever the reason, the underlying assumptions that inform many of the papers imply that it is possible to be an effective communicator without an explicit knowledge of theory. We would argue with this assumption. Of the texts mentioned in this knowledge review, some were identified in the York search.

In relation to the link between theory and practice, there were some papers that attempt to address this issue. For example, 2 papers and 1 book chapter look at the application of specific theories to the task of learning and teaching. Two further papers also attempt to link theory and practice in this way, but in areas that are more specialised. The paper by Dickson and Bamford is particularly impressive in its detailed overview of key issues in relation to learning and teaching of communication skills in social work education in the UK. Dickson and Bamford comment on the lack of research and publications on this. subject, which they broaden to include all publications relating to interpersonal skills:

> Interpersonal skills which enable the worker to engage meaningfully with the client, lie at the heart of effective social work practice ... it is, perhaps, surprising that relatively little has been published by way of a systematic exploration of current social work education/training provision in promoting skilled professional interaction.

The few articles on this subject identified in the CRD search seem to support this view. However, some difficulties may be due to differences in terminology. Dickson and Bamford are a case in point. Although these authors use the term interpersonal skills in their paper, they are, in effect, writing about communication skills. The same is true of some texts, such as Hargie et al. In other papers, interviewing skills is the preferred term. The use of different terms highlights a difficulty regularly encountered in the papers reviewed - and in social work generally. In order to address this problem of terminology, and the absence of clear definitions, it was agreed to add a glossary of terms to this knowledge review.

Similarly, there is little conformity in the range of approaches used to teach social work skills. Some appear to adopt quite different teaching methods, but with little reference to theory. These findings support research where newly qualified social work/probation practitioners were asked to name those theories they found useful, and were still using in their work. Over 80 theorists and theoretical approaches were identified from this question. These findings highlight the diversity of theories and methods taught, or learnt, on social work courses and the confusion that existed among the practitioners interviewed about what constitutes a theoretical approach. The seven main models included: Rogerian and other counselling approaches; task-centred social work; systemic ideas influencing especially family work/therapy; behavioural techniques; child development mainly based on Erikson's stages; psycho-social approaches; and crisis intervention. These findings are also in keeping with the emphasis on psychological perspectives found in the 16 papers read in this chapter.

This level of diversity makes it hard to conceptualise similarities and differences, and strengths and limitations, of the different approaches. adopted - a point taken up by Koprowska, who noted that: "The process of professional learning in the wider field is not fully understood; empirical studies are rare and methodological differences make comparison difficult". It also makes it difficult to identify whether the transfer of learning into - and across - different practice contexts has been effective.

A further drawback relates to the international flavour of the papers reviewed. Ten of the 16 articles reviewed describe the situation in North America , with only 3 articles referring to the UK. The remaining 3 papers relate to the educational context in Israel , to skills teaching in Germany and the international context from a Norwegian perspective. For these reasons, it has not been possible to draw any firm conclusions for England, and we suspect the same is true for Wales, Scotland and Northern Ireland.

Overall, psychological theories feature strongly in the papers reviewed. Humanistic psychology, informed by the client-centred theories of Carl Rogers , and psychosocial theories influenced by Freudian psychoanalytic theory, are the most commonly referenced theories. Where social work texts are cited, these references also reflect a more psychological perspective. Some authors attempt to redress this imbalance, calling for greater focus to be placed on social factors, such as "social development", or argue that there is a 'dissonance' when technical skills are taught within "humanist principles, without reference to any political context". These limitations withstanding, it is possible to group the papers into three general sections: psychology and counselling theory; communication and learning theory; and other theoretical perspectives.

Psychology and Counselling Theory

Much of the literature reviewed draws heavily on humanistic psychology and counselling theory. For example, several papers cite Carl Rogers and sometimes also Carkhuff. The influence of counselling can be seen in many of the texts cited in the articles reviewed. Hepworth and Larsden are cited in a range of papers , mainly because, it is argued, these authors "frame their analysis on an updated version of the Rogerian core conditions: empathy, authenticity, and respect". Fischer is also cited, largely for his teaching and writing on 'micro-skills', including empathy. The focus placed on empathy is interesting, and may reflect the fact that empathy is important in counselling, as well as social work.

Perhaps for this reason, this has led to a number of research studies on the effectiveness of empathy training in social work education. The work of Egan (the most recent edition of his text is cited here, as there are seven editions of the book) and his model of Problem Management and Opportunity Development, which is firmly located in the field of counselling theory, is also cited in several places and not always uncritically.

There is little attempt to analyse why humanistic psychology, particularly the work of Carl Rogers, is popular among social work students and practitioners. Similarly, there is little attempt to analyse critically the relevance of counselling theory to social work. As a result, insufficient attention is paid to the difficulties inherent when trying to apply concepts such as empathy to fieldwork settings, particularly statutory social work. It is again important to note that much of the literature referred to is more influential in North America than the UK.

Communication and learning theory

Under this heading are grouped references to communication and learning theory , with several authors referencing the work of Hargie. Communication theory draws on the principles of motor skills and transfers them into the context of social and communication skills. This perspective emphasises the 'technical' activity involved in communication. The particular importance of communication theory is its focus on 'micro-skills' that is, on the process of communication and the actual skills used in practice, but again, this theory draws heavily on psychology and counselling. For this reason, the skills it addresses are sometimes called 'micro-counselling' skills. One tension that arises from relying on communication theory is that it tends to see effective communication as a personal trait. Once a person has acquired this competence, it travels with that individual across different situations.

However, it is argued that "researchers have demonstrated that the ability to communicate competently is largely dependent on social context", as well as personal competence. If competence is context-specific in this way, this makes any analysis of competence and the transferability of skills a more complex issue than first assumed.

Learning theory and principles of behaviourism - assessment,. evaluation, feedback and reinforcement - feature in the literature as useful theoretical tools for facilitating the process of skills acquisition. Interestingly, adult learning theory focusing on experiential learning and the concept of 'learning by doing' - which might have been expected to inform the teaching of communication skills - is referenced in only 2 papers. Hansen explores 'learning by doing' and Schön's notions of 'reflection-in-action' in relation to the use of video in skills teaching. Koprowska, taking up some of the points made by Hansen, draws on a quote from Schön:

Perhaps, then, learning all forms of professional artistry depends, at least in part, on conditions similar to those created in the studios and conservatories: freedom to learn by doing in a setting relatively low in risk, with access to coaches who initiate students into the 'traditions of the calling' and help them, by 'the right kind of telling', to see on their own behalf and in their own way what they most need to see'.

Other theoretical perspectives

Another group of papers, written more recently, provide very clear and accessible accounts of specific theoretical frameworks and their application in practice. Edwards and Richards, Jessup and Rogerson and Koprowska warrant specific mention.

Edwards and Richards write on the application of 'relational/cultural theory' to learning and teaching in social work education. Based on the work of Jean Baker Miller and Janet Stiver , and others involved in the Stone Centre in Boston, US , their paper describes a psychosocial, relational perspective with regard to concepts such as mutual engagement, empathy and mutual empowerment. The paper argues that these concepts are not only important in the client-worker relationship but also in the student-teacher relationship:

> We believe that growth in social work education is the result of the student and teacher experiencing the dynamics of empowerment that come with mutual empathy. This perspective states that how students are taught will influence what they learn, and that this in turn will influence how they use this knowledge and understanding in practice.

The chapter by Jessup and Rogerson describes a postmodern and poststructural approach to teaching and practising interpersonal communication skills, arguing the case for teaching to be located in a 'political context'. Drawing on the work of Foucault , Freire , and Freire and Shor , concepts such as language and power are defined within this theoretical framework, and then applied to 'explicitly targeted exercises' to highlight their use in practice. The paper argues that certain concepts, such as those based on humanist principles, "have been constructed to produce an oppressive, rather than a liberating, social work practice".

Koprowska's article provides an overview of the skills training in social work education, both within universities and in practice settings. In a complex paper, Koprowska explores 'key concepts and methods' in relation to Agazarian's theory of 'living human systems', particularly 'systems-centred therapy', and how this process of learning and teaching can be applied within social work education. According to Koprowska, systems-centred therapy "deliberately structures group norms in order to reduce restraining forces and increase driving forces". The part played by 'predictable defences' needs to be 'undone' so that new information can be integrated in ways that enable students to "move away from personal preoccupations toward a process of professional discovery".

In addition, two other papers warrant mention. The first, by Hansen , provides an account of the work of Schön and Dreyfus and Dreyfus on direct skills acquisition, and how these theories can be used in teaching, with particular reference to the use of 'interactive video' as an 'instructional technology'. The second paper, by McMahon , is based on psychoanalytic theory and describes the application of these theories developed by Winnicott and Dockar-Drysdale to 'therapeutic communication' with children and young people.

No papers were identified that provided a commentary on how students view and experience the different models of teaching in relation to communication skills, or their preferences. Similarly, although Bricker-Jenkins and Lishman call for service users to be "considered the. primary experts", no papers explored the views of services users or carers on the competence of students and social work practitioners in relation to their communication skills. It is likely that this gap will be addressed in the requirements for the new social work degree.

Some papers touched on the transferability of skills from the classroom or 'laboratory' to practice settings, and between different client groups, settings and contexts. On the whole, this subject is not explored in great detail - an issue that is mentioned in the Brunel Practice Survey - "transferability of core learning is often assumed and opportunities for drawing this learning out were scarce". One exception is the article by Dickson and Bamford , who attempt to look at the "broader principles governing action". These authors call for greater crossover in terms of the design and delivery of social work (interpersonal) skills teaching.

Texts covering communication skills

The findings of the study revealed that of the 14 texts identified in the CRD electronic database search, only 2 references had social work in their title: Requirements for social work training and The social work skills workbook. Other texts identified as relevant to social work were targeted toward health professions , or covered more specialist areas, such as counselling or interviewing skills or communication skills in specific contexts. Of these texts, Collins and Collins Social skills training and the professional helper and Cournoyer The social work skills workbook have particular relevance to the learning and teaching of communication skills in social work. However, the tendency to target texts toward a more multi-professional readership made it difficult to assess the relevance of certain texts to social work.

However, from our knowledge and experience as academics, it was clear that more coverage of communication skills learning and teaching could be found in other textbooks than the limited number identified in the York electronic database search. As a result, we agreed to hand search key social work texts, using the same criteria adopted in the York search. Time restraints did not allow this search to be extensive but it highlighted some important texts and chapters. Lishman's Communication in social work is the only book included in the main body of the review that explicitly mentions both communication skills and social work in its title.

Other texts provide considerable coverage of communication skills, such as Kadushin and Kadushin , Thompson and Trevithick , while others focus on specific approaches to practice, such as counselling. Thompson provides a valuable account of the importance of verbal and non-verbal communication skills, and also writing and interviewing skills. A third range of generalist texts have specific sections dedicated to communication skills , and a fourth category located in the search focused on the importance of writing and presentation skills.

It has proved difficult to identify a coherent theoretical framework that informs the learning and teaching of communication skills in social work. The tenuous relationship between theory and practice in relation to social work skills, including communication skills, means that practitioners have tended to look to other theories outside social work to help them to understand human beings, and to acquire advanced or specialist skills.

Counselling theory and practice is particularly attractive in this regard, with its specific and accessible terminology. A closer relationship between theory and practice, linked to research, particularly in relation to learning and teaching communication skills, is a crucially important issue, and one that will no doubt be addressed in some detail in relation to the new social work degree.

Evidence on effectiveness of communication skills training

We turn next to review the literature relating to the second and third of four central questions:

— How have social work teachers designed and implemented programmes for learning communication skills?

— What impact, if any, have such programmes had?

The literature containing evidence on the content and effectiveness of communication skills training in social work education substantially overlaps the literature reviewed above. It has similar limitations, in particular the lack of a coherent body of evidence on which to draw and the preponderance of work from North America. By comparison the literature specific to the UK appears somewhat meagre.

The evidence can be grouped under two main headings. Narrative accounts provide detailed descriptions of the design and content of skills training programmes, with no attempt at systematic evaluation. Evaluative accounts typically contain a more limited description of programme content and rationale, focusing instead on the measurement of outcomes. The literature that deals with the recent surge in the use of computer-aided learning (CAL) has tended to include an evaluative dimension to it, although the successful transferability of the transatlantic experience to the UK context is by no means guaranteed.

One further point deserves emphasis. In the narrative and evaluative literature identified in this review there was a notable absence of any reference to training students in written communication skills. The importance of this area of work cannot be denied, and points to the need for further work to be undertaken. This crucial limitation to the scope of this study is admitted at the outset. .

Design and implementation

Taken together, the narrative and evaluative accounts give an overview of different approaches to the learning and teaching of communication skills. The programmes described vary in length and intensity and involve students at different stages of undergraduate or postgraduate social work courses. Most focus on the development of basic interpersonal skills in interviewing and combine formal input from an instructor with experiential learning, usually in small group sessions with role-play and video. Behavioural methods are widely used, with systematic feedback and reinforcement provided by tutors or peers. In the earlier literature, the training programmes focus on developing empathic communication the ability to grasp the meaning of communication in terms of content and affect and to respond appropriately. Micro-skills training, with its emphasis on the processes of communication, is prominent in the more recent literature.

The programmes that focus on empathy share a common theoretical basis in the work of Carl Rogers, Carkhuff and other counselling theorists. However, substantial variation is apparent in the content of individual programmes. For example, Toseland and Spielberg focus on the skills required to "facilitate client self-exploration and action: empathy; genuineness; respect; concreteness; confrontation; self-disclosure; warmth; immediacy; potency and self-actualisation". Nerdrum and Lundquist work with their students on: tuning in; decentering; active listening; empathic communication; confrontation and understanding of client resistance.

Nerdrum and Lundquist's thoughtful and relatively recent article is also an indication that the empathy-based approach to skills training continues to develop. Bondareva et al provides another recent example of professional training that is directed towards developing the personality of the social work student, but with limited information about programme content and method. Non-behavioural approaches to developing empathy, such as structured meditation and experiential focusing , that aim to increase the student's perceptual awareness, are found only in the earlier literature.

Micro-skills training, which is concerned with improving the student's mastery of the processes of communication, offers an alternative highly structured approach. Dickson and Mullan describe sessions on each of the seven interviewing skills: non-verbal communication; questioning; reflecting; listening; explaining; set induction and closure. This approach. is particularly associated in the UK with the work of Hargie and colleagues.

While the evaluative literature provides only limited information on the experiences of those involved in training, the narrative literature is reflective in tone and contains rich insights into the rewards and challenges of different approaches for both teachers and learners. It also includes several examples of innovative approaches to the learning and teaching of communication skills in social work education in the UK. For example, Rachman describes a series of workshops on interviewing intended to promote student-centred learning. Students were actively involved in the planning, organisation and running of workshops that focused on their experiences in practice. Another imaginative response to the challenge of linking theory to practice is the use of large group role-play, as described by Moss.

This technique seeks to create a learning environment in which students can explore both structural and personal issues and dilemmas. In doing so it addresses the criticism that much interpersonal skills training is divorced from the critique of structural oppression that is central to social work education. Koprowska is concerned with the question of learning style and how to create a suitable learning environment for skill development. She provides an intriguing account of a workshop-based course on interview skills to demonstrate how Agazarian's theory of living human systems may be used to maximise opportunities for student learning.

Impact of Training

What has been the impact, if any, of programmes for the learning of communication skills in social work education? Here, too, the evidence from the literature is often unclear. Overall, it would seem that behavioural approaches to communication skills training are helpful, when compared with formal classroom teaching alone or with opportunistic practice settings. They are generally well received by students, although reactions may vary among students with differing levels of practice experience. However, there is also some evidence that behavioural approaches may have potentially negative effects, as in the finding by Barber that training in specific micro-skills may increase student self-awareness, while reducing the student's client awareness. However, the findings from the literature should be treated with caution.

Despite efforts at systematic evaluation, methodological problems abound. As summarised by Dickson and Bamford , these include the use of single group post-test only designs , and the absence of random allocation to experimental and control groups.

There are indications in the literature that student learning persists beyond the end of training. A well-designed study by Nerdrum found positive evidence that the effect of communication skills training is maintained over a follow-up period of 18 months. However, this study also indicated that the development of skilfulness was slow and dependent on specific training of therapeutic skills. Evidence relating to the yet more important question of whether student learning is transferred into practice is much less encouraging.

An investigation by Kopp and Butterfield of student interview skills, before and after micro-skills training and subsequently with clients in practice settings, found an increased use of closed questions in the field, suggesting that student skills may have deteriorated in certain respects. Another much larger study by Collins and Bogo , investigating the transferability of laboratory-based learning of interview skills to encounters with service users, yielded similar findings. They looked at the communication of the basic skills of empathy, warmth and genuineness. They found a significant improvement in these skills when they tested students, through role-play interviews and a written test, before and after skills training.

However, when the same students were assessed through tape-recordings of interviews with users, while on placement, the improvement was not sustained. The authors point to methodological issues, such as differences between the laboratory and field settings and in the measures used to assess skills in role-play and client interviews, which may explain the lack of skill transfer. Nevertheless they conclude that a more systematic competency-based approach to both the assessment and development of skills in the field would facilitate the transfer of laboratory-based learning. This message is supported by Dickson and Bamford in their comprehensive review of the problem of skill transfer.

The philosophy of 'train and hope' is, they argue, hopelessly inadequate. Instead attention should be paid to the content of training programmes to ensure relevance to the workplace, and to the student's personal attributes, such as personality and learning style. At the same time the role of the practice teacher in maximising college-based learning should be extended.

The definition and measurement of outcomes presents substantial difficulties for the evaluation of skills training programmes. Typically,. training outcomes are measured in terms of changes in the student rather than in service users. Although studies such as Kopp and Butterfield and Collins and Bogo have attempted to assess changes in practice with service users, the outcome measures used relate to the quality of the student's communication with the service user, not the impact of that communication on the service user's behaviour or quality of life.

A further criticism of many evaluative studies is that the effect of training is measured soon after it has ended and with no follow-up. Another potential weakness in many studies is that the training and assessment of students depends on a single scale, such as Carkhuff 's overall index of therapeutic communication, so that the effect of training is likely to be exaggerated. The choices available to social work educators for the learning and teaching of communication skills have been further extended by the development of IT resources.

Contribution of IT and Multi-media Programs

The authors are acutely aware that the use of IT has now pervaded social work process and practice. It has also enriched much contemporary pedagogy, where there is a burgeoning literature now available. In social work practice, the electronic base of communication within and across professional boundaries has transformed practice skills. There are also current developments in online service provision that also raise important issues in communication skills.

However, much of the literature that deals with these important developments falls outside the search terms for this particular review. This indicates the urgent need for a more comprehensive review of both narrative and evaluative studies of IT developments in the field of communication skills. Within the literature generated by the CRD search for this study, a key question concerned the contribution that such resources can make to the actual teaching of communication skills.

In the area of interpersonal skills training, the use of videotape and audiotape already has a long history, and the literature offers some evaluation of these 'practice skills aids'. It is not surprising, however, that the IT revolution has seen a surge in the development of imaginative resources available to teacher and student alike.

Hansen et al , for example, assess the effectiveness of a multi-media communications skills training programme focusing on developing students' skills in 'paraphrasing' and ' perception checking', in order to enhance their professional listening skills. Engen and Dawson evaluate an interactive CD Rom 'designed to provide realistic situations in which students can learn and evaluate their micro-counselling skills' in a program based in the University of Iowa. Resnick explores ways in which a complex multi-media package involving graphics, text, video images and audio could be used to develop students' listening skills. Brawley adopts a somewhat different approach in his article, where he describes how he teaches social work students to develop their advocacy skills through the mass media.

At this point it is helpful briefly to highlight some of the pedagogic assumptions underlying these developments. First, there is the assumption that the benefits from these often expensive and time-consuming developments will outweigh more traditional methods of teaching communication skills. Second, there is an uncritical assumption that 'experiential is best'. Third, the application of key underpinning knowledge, or a theoretical framework for such developments, is rarely articulated. Fourth, it is assumed that skilled tutors are needed to get the best out of students using such packages.

The literature frequently reflects the enthusiastic championing of IT-based approaches. Resnick , for example, proclaims that "The computer is infinitely patient, consistent, non-judgmental, and always supportive of students learning at their own pace and in their own place". The overall message drawn from the literature reviewed in this study, however, suggests that it is wise to be a little circumspect when looking at these developments from a UK perspective.

There are four main themes about these developments that have been identified. First, the majority of the literature comes from the US and Canada, where Hansen et al report an increase over a 20-year period (1977- 97), from 1% to 70% in computer-based instruction. The strong 'learner-autonomy' ethos is cited as a major advantage in such programmes whereby the student can control the pace, timing and intensity of their learning. 'Interactivity' is seen to be an essential ingredient in helping students develop their skills. There is a general consensus in the literature. reviewed that a majority of students placed some value on this style of learning.

Second, the transferability of such resources into a UK context is clearly an important issue when it comes to the fine-tuning of social work skills to specific contexts. This is an issue, of course, which also affects hard copy workbooks and textbooks such as Evans et al , Collins and Collins , and

Cournoyer. It is in the immediate and focused responses, in simulated as well as live contexts, that the quality of a student's skills is really enhanced.

Third, the IT packages currently available, including Procare's Interpersonal Skills CAL package , reviewed in Thompson and MacFadden , all make the point that best practice will use such programmes to support, enhance and consolidate, not replace, face-to-face teaching.

Fourth, IT packages are expensive in time, money and developmental expertise, and often have a limited shelf life. Hansen et al , for example, report that their multi-media package took 30 people over two years to design and produce. Careful decisions have to be made about whether the outcomes from such packages justify the initial - and updating -outlay costs.

In seeking to evaluate these developments, the strongest note of caution is issued by MacFadden et al. They explore a set of issues and questions about how students are enabled to learn through such resources, and importantly, what the barriers are to learning through IT programs. These authors raise some crucially important issues when they discuss the 'human face of online education'. They argue that the literature which seeks to evaluate online learning rarely offers "any significant focus on the subjective experience of the most important partner in this new educational process - the learner".

They make a significant contribution towards understanding the emotional impact of such programs on the learner and the facilitator. It is in both the student's and facilitator's interest that 'learning anxiety' is reduced, and that the program encourages early success for everyone involved. It is often assumed that instructions given online will be easily understood and followed by students, whereas in fact it can be "extremely difficult to be totally clear and encompassing in explaining a task in written instruction". Facilitators have to grapple with issues like "getting lost in [cyber] space; what does 'bored' look like on-line? [and] how do theories of group dynamics apply to an on-line group?". Anyone involved in developing or seeking to make use of CAL would do well to explore the issues which MacFadden et al raise with thoughtful attention: unless they are dealt with properly, a successful outcome to a CAL program is likely to be very difficult to achieve.

Skills laboratories

Skills laboratories offer opportunities for simulated practice, with facilities for feedback often through video recording. With the likely development of skills laboratories with the new social work degree, it is instructive to review the literature to explore how some more familiar 'tried and tested' techniques have been evaluated. Mackey and Sheingold , for example, discuss the use of video laboratory work in Massachusetts to help clinical social work trainees to develop their empathy skills. Small groups of 4-5 trainees meet with a clinical instructor throughout the year, and each trainee is both interviewer and interviewee at least once in the group's programme.

The interviews last 20 minutes, with an hour being given over to feedback, discussion and analysis. The creation of a safe learning environment where students can take risks, and where the tutor is able to facilitate a creative learning environment, is of paramount importance. It is 'out of the question' to let students simply 'go and play': the technique needs skilled and trained tutors who are able to use the equipment creatively and effectively. This view is confirmed by Vinton and Harrington and by Pope , who describes the tutor's role as supporting and encouraging individual learning and small group work process. By contrast, however, Rachman reports that with video playback work, students felt more at ease and learned more when a tutor was not present.

In this context, an important caveat raised by Collins and Bogo about the issue of transferability mentioned earlier in this study, deserves to be repeated:

> Mastery of skill in a laboratory does not necessarily mean that students will be able to utilize those skills ... with clients.
>
> They found that,
>
> . ... a significant improvement in skill level for the students from the beginning of the laboratory to the end of the laboratory. However, students did not transfer their learned skills ... to the field....

This finding, albeit some 20 years ago, raises a fundamental issue about all classroom-based communication skills work, and its transferability to practice. In the new social work degree, with its emphasis on service user and carer participation, it may be that this bridge will be more effectively crossed in future. Future evaluative work, however, will be essential.

Narrative and evaluative concerns

The learning and teaching of communication skills in social work education in the UK has not been widely written up or evaluated. This is particularly the case with the multi-media approaches that are being developed in the UK.

Instead, much of the evaluative literature is from North America and is concerned with the learning and teaching of interview skills. Although there is evidence that such training increases student skilfulness, it is often unclear whether these skills are maintained and transferred to work with service users.

A general weakness in the evaluative literature is the lack of attention to outcomes in work with service users and to how these may be defined and measured. The need to integrate communication skills training with practice learning is a recurrent theme. Innovative approaches that integrate the development of communication skills with other aspects of the social work curriculum, and seek to ensure an environment for learning, are now more in evidence in the UK literature. These require systematic evaluation to assess their effectiveness for future practice.

Likewise, a comparison between an IT program approach and a more face-to-face experiential style, as encouraged by recent skills laboratory developments, would be particularly illuminating for the development of the new degree. We need to know not only what is the most effective use of resources, but also what prepares students best for the demands of their future social work careers. Finally, as indicated in the introduction to this chapter, there is a need for further work into evaluating the effectiveness of training in written communication skills.

Meeting Particular Communication Needs

The CRD search produced several articles that help students and practitioners to work with user groups with particular communication difficulties. Most of the articles are narrative accounts of short training courses in a range of settings and with a specific focus, for example, bereavement, challenging behaviour etc. Usually the formal input was described with examples of encounters between professionals and service users, which conveyed the central importance of communication in the delivery and experience of care services.

Learning disabilities have attracted some research interest. Dobson et al describe a training programme which provides 'direct support skills' to adults with profound learning disabilities. Active participation of care staff with individual service users is video-recorded and assessed by the staff group. The learning of staff members is reinforced by observing their own interactions, the interventions of other staff members and the systematic feedback from the group. Boyle describes the Sexual Attitude Reassessment Programme (SARS) used to explore and engender the skills needed to enable service users and care staff to discuss sexuality. This programme utilised films, lectures and small as well as large group discussions focused on sexuality and individuals with disability. Sutton and Thurman focus on a training pack which provides factual information about 'challenging behaviour' and engages users through life story books, objects and pictures that signal intent.

Work with older adults has also been evidenced. Dreher describes an earlier course that integrates knowledge of difficulties and strengths related to this life stage with a wide range of relevant communication skills and devices. Biographies of users are compiled by students and given to the user to provide new insights and perspectives on their lives and life experiences. Bender et al describe a training course about the roles that women with dementia and other women of various ages have occupied during their lifetime. They outline the benefits that users and students obtained in the process of exploring the life roles of each participant.

Benefits listed include being listened to, given space to talk, positive student learning and improved anti-discriminatory practice.

There were a number of articles that look at specific contexts. For example, Webster et al use a multi-disciplinary approach and account for the organisational challenges that arise while developing a creative curriculum for working with substance misuse. The project involves academic and practice collaboration at a local level and emphasises the development of effective verbal and non-verbal communication and improved self-knowledge. Fieweger describes a well-designed programme in a hospice setting. The article details the programme set up to support patients and family through the bereavement process. It describes different stages of awareness of impending death and the grief process. It also outlines the various skills and devices used by volunteers to engage the patient and the family. Mattern and Camp present a case study of teaching care staff a few essential phrases in the foreign language employed by the service users with whom they work. They report slight increases in the interactions and reactions of carers and users over a three-month period of their programme.

The above needs may be seen as personal, but social workers also address particular needs that are more social. Brawley adopts a wider view by showing how social workers can be trained in media advocacy with a view to correcting distorted messages about vulnerable people given by the press, developing policies and services and relaying important messages to large target audiences. Robinson draws attention to the lack of information about inter-racial communication. She contends that research is 'eurocentric' in theory, method and focus. Her article is written in the UK and from a black perspective. She suggests guidelines for social work trainers dealing with inter-racial communication. Zapf look at the dearth of recent literature in the US about cross-cultural practice. He explores the use of magic as a tool to explore uncertainty and promote cross-cultural practice.

Rosenfield explores what at first glance is a specialised skill of applying telephone technology to counselling. She has pioneered a great deal of the UK telephone 'hotline' industry. Her article argues for "the legitimisation of the telephone as a valid means by which to deliver counseling", but also raises issues of 'net' meetings between counsellor and client, and text-phone work with deaf clients.

More generally,. however, there are implications for social work training where it is often simply assumed that students will be competent and skilful telephone users in their professional role. This is an important area where training could be developed in the skills laboratory context. Generally the articles in this grouping produced examples of particular settings, specific user groups and specific techniques and provided good descriptions about the practical arrangements in terms of length and timing, content and follow-up arrangements. Many programmes involved small numbers of users and required significant resources of staff time. Staff used words, questions, symbols, pictures, life storybooks and so forth to develop and encourage the communication skills of users.

Additionally they communicated with colleagues to check their learning and to ensure that the training programme was on track. The lack of systematic evaluation was extremely disappointing. Many papers contained no evaluation. Those that included some evaluation usually focused on the process, the benefits or products and mainly from the perspective of facilitators. There was a distinct lack of emphasis on systematic evaluation of data related to outcomes. Only two of the articles in this group involved some degree of rigorous evaluation of outcomes. Recommendations were usually concerned with repeating, amending or expanding of the programmes.

The views of service users were usually absent despite the emphasis on active participation and collaboration with service users. There was no real certainty about the user's awareness of the purpose of communication, and the meaning of the encounter was usually interpreted by professionals. There were no reports of measurement of skills prior to and at the end of the intervention. Where there was reported evidence of an increase in staff skills, no evidence was produced about the sustainability or transference of these skills to other situations. The articles from education settings provided information on theory and suggested content for training programmes, but they did not report on actual programmes and no attention was given to student characteristics and potential.

The absence of a coherent body of literature is itself interesting. It could be due to the fact that pedagogic research is not highly valued in Research Exercise Assessment (RAE) rating and, therefore, there is less incentive for academics to work in this area. Or it may be due to the fact that research funding for a substantive piece of pedagogic research is difficult to acquire. However, it is important to note that the Economic and Social Research Council (ESRC) has recently made funding available for pedagogic research. This must be welcomed if it leads to rigorous research and to a greater focus on helping students to learn how to work with user groups with particular communication difficulties.

Key messages

The theoretical underpinning in relation to the learning and teaching of communication skills is underdeveloped. For example, there is little coherence in the literature to assist educators to teach effectively, and little coverage of students' different learning styles. These differences are reflected in the divergent range of models identified by the Brunel Practice Survey and also in research undertaken by Marsh and Triseliotis.

In light of the requirements of the new degree in relation to the learning and teaching of communication skills, several aspects require particular attention:

— there is an absence of literature that addresses service user involvement in, and perspectives on, the learning and teaching of communication skills;

— greater focus is needed on the importance of transcultural communication skills given the limited literature and research in this area;

— encouragement needs to be given to enable practitioners to contribute to teaching/learning in all aspects of practice, particularly those areas such as transcultural communication skills, where there is a serious lack of literature and research;

— there is scope for more work to be done on the learning and teaching of specific communication skills associated with specific theoretical approaches;

— the lack of a 'common language' means that greater rigour is needed when using such terms as generalist, specialist and advanced practice skills, micro-skills and macro-skills; interventions, and so on;

— the processes involved in teaching communication skills require as much attention as the content of the teaching;

— evaluative studies which focus on the learning and teaching of interviewing and listening skills suggest that the improvements made in simulated settings do not automatically transfer to practice settingswith service users. The integration of communication skills training with practice learning is seen as crucial here;

— the increasing use of computer-based programs and skills laboratories is described in the literature, but the limited evaluation of such resources suggests that they are best used to support face-to-face teaching rather than as 'stand-alone' training in communication skills;

—the relative paucity of evaluative literature indicates that there is an urgent need to develop a robust methodology, particularly with regard to defining and measuring the effectiveness of communication skills with service users.

Challenges of the Future

In light of the requirements of the new degree, the learning of communication skills needs to be seen as a priority in social work education. Although this knowledge review has not been able to identify from the literature reviewed a unified body of knowledge on which such teaching programmes can be based, it has highlighted those aspects that need further attention.

First, the practical constraints on this project made it impossible for the authors to address three significant aspects of the literature generated by the CRD search:

— the literature on learning and teaching of communication skills in other sectors such as medicine, nursing and allied health professionals;

— the literature on improving communications skills of users;

— the learning and teaching of communication skills in relation to working interprofessionally.

It is anticipated that further work will be commissioned by SCIE to examine these issues. Second, it is recognised that there is far greater expertise in existence than is reflected in the literature. The findings of the Brunel Practice Survey **33** indicate that there is a considerable amount of innovative practice being undertaken in this field that is, as yet, barely covered in the literature. It is hoped, therefore, that this knowledge review can serve as a catalyst to educators in two ways: by encouraging educators to write for publication their knowledge and experience on this aspect of education, and to address the gaps in existing knowledge by undertaking research in the areas identified in the review's key messages.

Third, the theoretical knowledge base that underpins the learning and teaching of communication skills needs to be made more explicit, adopting the same academic rigour used in other areas of social work research and practice theory. The review was enriched by the international scope of the articles provided by the search, but the transferability of much of the material to the UK context is far from straightforward. Furthermore, more research is needed on the transferability of communication skills learning and teaching from the university to practice contexts, and across different settings and service user groups.

Finally, there is an urgent need to undertake a comprehensive and critical review of the contribution that IT is making to the development of communication skills within social work process, practice and pedagogy. If these challenges can be met, there is the potential for the learning and teaching of communication skills in social work to be built on firm foundations – an essential prerequisite for effective teaching, learning and practice.

Instructional Design

The field of instructional design developed in the 1960s and early 1970s at a time when behaviorism still dominated mainstream psychology. ID shared those behaviorist roots and at the time was closer to mainstream psychology in the U. S. ID theorists such as Gagné, Briggs, Merrill, and Scandura all were educational psychologists. With the cognitive revolution of the 1970s, instructional psychology differentiated itself from ID and drifted more to the cognitive mainstream, leaving ID relatively isolated with concerns of design. In a review of instructional psychology in 1981, Lauren Resnick observed:

> An interesting thing has happened to instructional psychology. It has become part of the mainstream of research on human cognition, learning, and development. For about 20 years the number of psychologists devoting attention to instructionally relevant questions has been gradually increasing. In the past 5 years this increase has accelerated so that it is now difficult to draw a clear line between instructional psychology and the main body of basic research on complex cognitive processes. Instructional psychology is no longer basic psychology applied to education. It is fundamental research on the processes of instruction and learning.

In her review, Resnick acknowledged that mainstream instructional psychologists had focused on issues of performance modeling and cognitive task analysis, neglecting the challenge of devising effective instructional strategies, models, and interventions. Even so, she did not look to the ID community to fill the need because "Instructional design theory..., which is directly concerned with prescribing interventions, has developed without much reference to cognitive psychology". Hence, she excluded ID theory entirely from her review. Of course, the ID community was active during this time, with even some attempt at integrating cognitive psychology into their methods --Resnick and other mainstream psychologists just weren't reading them! This polarization between ID and psychology continued through the 1980s. In spite of efforts to move ID into the cognitive mainstream, psychologists and designers continued to move in different circles and speak somewhat different languages. Psychologists viewed designers with suspicion because of the eclectic and ad hoc nature of the ID theory base and because of the field's concern for stimulus design over cognitive processes. Likewise, the ID literature often ignored developments in cognitive theory, resulting in theory that was generally divorced from state-of-the-art learning theory.

Only recently, with the vigorous dialogue on constructivism and situated learning, have psychologists and designers resumed a substantive conversation. Psychologists such as Bransford, Perkins, Scardamalia, and Lesgold, who have taken on the challenge of design, have run up against many of the same problems addressed by traditional ID theories. At the same time, the perspectives of psychologists have stimulated reflection and renewal within the ID community. The net result of this interplay is a renewed recognition of the importance of design, as well as an array of new designs that take into account new technologies and theories of learning.

Role of Teaching Models in Research

Like other scientists, instructional psychologists develop theories and models describing the world, then use accepted methods of inquiry to test and revise those theories. Examples of appropriate research methods include controlled experiments in laboratory settings as well as ethnographic and qualitative studies in field settings. Another legitimate method of testing out concepts and strategies is to develop a prototype teaching model and assess its overall effectiveness in different settings. A teaching model incorporates a complex array of learning/ instructional factors into a single working system.

The development and tryout of practical teaching models would not normally come to mind as a method of "research," yet surely such design and implementation efforts yield important new knowledge about the viability of cognitive theories and models. Perhaps such practical projects could be termed "inquiry" even if they do not fit the traditional connotation of "research." When researchers become interested in the problem of how people learn complex subject matters in realistic learning settings, practical tryout of programs and methods fills a role that no amount of theorizing or isolated-factor research can provide.

Teaching models can derive from direct empirical observation. Collins and Stevens closely observed teachers who used a Socratic dialogue approach and, based on the observed patterns, developed an instructional framework for inquiry teaching. Duffy (in press) developed a hypermedia tool to help preservice teachers to develop instructional strategies. The tool displays real-life segments of master teachers' lessons, then offers critiques from a number of perspectives, including those of the observed teachers. It also provides an electronic notepad for each preservice teacher to reflect on strategies used in the teaching episodes. While one could argue that Duffy's work is merely a neutral tool for displaying observed teaching performances, the tool embodies an underlying teaching model that is heavily grounded in actual teaching performances. Such "bottom-up" approaches can complement the heavy influence of "top-down" learning theory as a basis for the design of teaching models.

In summary, the development of teaching models constitutes a unique combination of theory construction and empirical testing. Theoretical abstractions must be carried to a new level of specificity as they become instantiated into an effective teaching program. At the same time, promising theory must be tested against the demands of real-world settings. Thus the development and testing of teaching models helps triangulate findings from more traditional research methods and assures a relevance to the practice of teaching.

Improving Traditional Instrction: Cognitive Load Theory

For a number of years, John Sweller, an Australian psychologist from the University of New South Wales, has examined instructional implications of a model of memory called "cognitive load theory." Cognitive load theory is based on a straightforward reading of information-processing concepts of memory, schema development, and automaticity of procedural knowledge:

— Human working memory is limited--we can only keep in mind a few things at a time. This poses a fundamental constraint on human performance and learning capacity.

— Two mechanisms to circumvent the limits or working memory are:

— Schema acquisition, which allows us to chunk information into meaningful units, and

— Automation of procedural knowledge.

The first mechanism deals primarily with processing and understanding information; the second deals with the acquisition of skills. Each mechanism helps us overcome the limits of working memory by drawing on our long-term memories, which are very detailed and powerful.

Sweller's model of instructional design is based upon these concepts:

1. Our limited working memories make it difficult to assimilate multiple elements of information simultaneously.

2. When multiple information elements interact, they must be presented simultaneously. This imposes a heavy cognitive load upon the learner of the information and threatens successful learning.

3. High levels of element "interactivity" and their resulting cognitive load can be inherent in the content--e.g., learning language grammar inherently involves more element interactivity than simple vocabulary learning. However, weak methods of presentation and instruction may result in unnecessarily high overhead. An example would be to present a student a figure whose understanding requires repeated consultation of the text. The extra work required in decoding and translating the figure competes with the content for

precious working-memory resources as the learner attempts to comprehend the material.

Cognitive load theory leads to some specific predictions for student learning:

— Simple content--i.e., content with relatively few intrinsic interactive elements--is not threatened by weak instructional methods. Learners are generally able to fit the demands of content and instruction within their working memories in such cases.

— Content containing high levels of interactivity among its elements cannot be learned effectively through weak instructional methods--that is, methods that require extra processing by learners. The demands of content and/or the method exceed the limits of the learner's working memory and learning does not occur.

Sweller's cognitive load theory has led to a number of instructional prescriptions, including:

— Carefully analyze the attention demands of instruction. Sweller's method defines "elements" and then counts the number of elements in instructional messages. Processing troubles arise when the learner must attend to too many different elements at the same time.

— Use single, coherent representations. These should allow the learner to focus attention rather than split attention between two places, e.g., between a diagram and the text or even between a diagram with labels not located close to their referents.

— Eliminate redundancy. Redundant information between text and diagram have been shown to decrease learning.

— Provide for systematic problem-space exploration instead of conventional repeated practice.

— In multimedia instruction, present animation and audio narration (and/or text descriptions) simultaneously rather than sequentially.

— Provide worked examples as alternatives to conventional problem-based instruction.

Examples

Conventional models of instruction in many domains involve the presentation of a principle, concept, or rule, followed by extensive practice on problems applying the rule. This approach at first glance seems like commonsense--providing ample skills practice is "learning by doing." However, cognitive load theory suggests that such instructional approaches may actually be hurting learners' understanding of the subject matter.

Sweller and Cooper examined the cognitive-load effects of methods for teaching algebra to high-school students. They hypothesized that when learners confront a conventional end-of-chapter practice exercise, they devote too much attention to the problem goal and to relatively weak search strategies such as means-end analysis. Students already know how to use general search strategies to solve problems; what they lack is the specific understanding of how cases relate to the general rule.

Sweller and Cooper hypothesized that learners might benefit from studying worked examples until they have "mastered" them, rather than working on conventional practice problems as soon as they have "obtained a basic familiarity with new material". The authors developed an alternative teaching model that emphasized the study of worked examples. After learners acquire a basic understanding of the algebraic principle, they study a series of examples; then the teacher answers any questions the learners have. When the learners indicate they understand the problems, they are required to explain the goal of each sample problem and to identify the mathematical operation used in each step of the problem. The teacher provides assistance to any learners who have difficulty with the questions. Then the learners complete similar problems, repeating them until they are solved with no errors; if too much time elapses, the teacher provides the answer.

Sweller and Cooper found that in the worked-examples model, acquisition of knowledge was significantly less time-consuming than in the conventional practice-based model. Furthermore, learners required significantly less time to solve similar problems (i.e., problems identical in structure) and made significantly fewer errors than did their counterparts. There were no significant group differences in solving novel problems. Thus learning was more efficient with no discerned loss in effectiveness. The authors concluded that "the use of worked examples may redirect attention away from the problem goal and toward problem-state configurations and their associated moves".

Sweller summarizes his position toward problem solving and learning by arguing that:

a. both schema acquisition and rule automation are the building blocks of skilled problem-solving performance...;

b. paradoxically, a heavy emphasis on conveying problem solving is not the best way to acquire schemas or facilitate rule automation because the means-end strategy commonly used focuses attention inappropriately and imposes a heavy cognitive load;

c. alternatives to conventional problem solving such as...worked examples must be carefully analyzed and, if necessary, modified to ensure that they, too, do not inappropriately direct attention and impose a heavy cognitive load; and

d. for the same reasons as for Point C, the format of instructional materials should be organized to minimize the need for students to attend to and mentally integrate disparate sources of information.

Sweller's critics might claim that students under the worked-example treatment were indeed actively engaging in problem-solving and practice activities, but that the nature of the practice shifted from traditional word problems to the study of worked examples. Instead of engaging in a multi-task activity (e.g., translating the word problem into one or more formulas, and performing calculations), the task narrowed to articulating the goal of the worked example and the appropriate mathematical operation. Sweller would likely agree with the critic. The point of the research is to suggest that not all "problem-solving" activities are equally effective. Some problem-solving activities actually leave learners at a loss, forcing them to resort to "weak" problem-solving methods--which they already know--rather than "strong" or domain-specific methods--which they are trying to learn. Bereiter and Scardamalia discuss this issue:

> In novel situations, where no strong methods have been devised, weak methods are all anyone has. We use them all the time, whenever we are stumped. But just because everyone uses them, could hardly survive without doing so, and therefore practices them extensively, there is reason to question the value of teaching them. Teaching problem-solving skills may be an illusion, like teaching babies to talk.

If our goal is to teach students certain well-defined domains such as algebra or physics, then giving them problems requiring extensive use of "weak" methods may be counterproductive and may even interfere with learning the domain.

One limitation of the Sweller and Cooper study was that only indirect inferences could be made concerning learners' cognitive processes. Chi and her colleagues addressed this issue in the area of college-level physics. They analyzed the think-aloud protocols of good and poor problem solvers to identify the cognitive processes learners used in studying worked examples in physics. Learners in the study did not differ significantly in their prior knowledge of physics; instead, good and poor problem solvers were identified by their performance on objective tests.

Chi's worked examples differed from those used by Sweller and Cooper in significant ways. Sweller and Cooper presented worked-example sheets which were not part of a text and which included no verbal commentary. By contrast, the physics examples were part of the text and included step-by-step verbal commentary, although the learners had to infer the "why's and wherefore's" of each step.

Self-explanations were one kind of student response to the worked examples. "A self-explanation is a comment about an example statement that contains domain-relevant information over and above what was stated in the example line itself". Chi et al. found that good problem solvers generated more self-explanations than poor problem solvers and that poor problem solvers used the examples rotely as prompts for solving subsequent problems.

In an intervention study, Chi et al.found that high-ability and average-ability students benefited equally from being prompted to generate self-explanations. This finding counters other research on strategy training, which has found that such training generally benefits low-ability students while it doesn't benefit and may even interfere with the performance of high-ability students. These discrepant findings might be partially explained by the fact that the earlier studies tended to teach skills rather than strategies.

Cognitive Apprenticeship Model

Collins, Brown, and colleagues developed an instructional model derived from the metaphor of the apprentice working under the master craftsperson in traditional societies, and from the way people seem to learn in everyday informal environments. The cognitive apprenticeship model rests on a somewhat romantic conception of the "ideal" apprenticeship as a method of becoming a master in a complex domain. In contrast to the classroom context, which tends to remove knowledge from its sphere of use, Collins and Brown recommend establishing settings where worthwhile problems can be worked with and solved. The need for a problem-solving orientation to education is apparent from the difficulty schools are having in achieving substantial learning outcomes.

Emulating the best features of apprenticeships is needed because, as Gott noted, lengthy periods of apprenticeship are becoming a rarity in industrial and military settings. She termed this phenomenon the "lost apprenticeship." She noted the effects of the increased complexity and automation of production systems. First, the need is growing for high levels of expertise in supervising and using automated work systems; correspondingly, the need for entry levels of expertise is declining. Workers on the job are more and more expected to be flexible problem solvers; human intervention is often most needed at points of breakdown or malfunction. At these points, the expert is called in. Experts, however narrow the domain, do more than apply canned job aids or troubleshooting algorithms; rather, they draw on the considerable knowledge they have internalized and use it to flexibly solve problems in real time.

Gott's second observation relates to training opportunities. Now, at a time when more problem-solving expertise is needed due to the complexity of systems, fewer on-the-job training opportunities exist for entry-level workers. There is often little or no chance for beginning workers to acclimatize themselves to the job, and workers very quickly are expected to perform like seasoned professionals. True apprenticeship experiences are becoming relatively rare. Gott calls this dilemma--more complex job requirements with less time on the job to learn--the "lost" apprenticeship and argues for the critical need for cognitive apprenticeships and simulation-type training to help workers develop greater problem-solving expertise.

Features of Cognitive Apprenticeship

The Collins-Brown model of cognitive apprenticeship incorporates the following instructional strategies or components.

1. Content: Teach tacit, heuristic knowledge as well as textbook knowledge. Collins et al. refer to four kinds of knowledge:

- Domain knowledge is the conceptual, factual, and procedural knowledge typically found in textbooks and other instructional materials. This knowledge is important, but often is insufficient to enable students to approach and solve problems independently.
- Heuristic strategies are "tricks of the trade" or "rules of thumb" that help people narrow solution paths while solving a problem. Experts usually pick up heuristic knowledge indirectly through repeated problem-solving practice; slower learners usually fail to acquire this subtle knowledge and never develop competence. There is evidence to believe, however, that at least some heuristic knowledge can be made explicit and represented in a teachable form.
- Control strategies are required for students to monitor and regulate their problem-solving activity. Control strategies have monitoring, diagnostic, and remedial components; this kind of knowledge is often termed metacognition.
- Learning strategies are strategies for learning; they may be domain, heuristic, or control strategies. Inquiry teaching to some extent directly models expert learning strategies.

2. *Situated learning*: Teach knowledge and skills in contexts that reflect the way the knowledge will be useful in real life. Brown, Collins, and Duguid argue for placing all instruction within "authentic" contexts that mirror real-life problem-solving situations. Collins is less forceful, moving away from real-life requirements and toward problem-solving situations:

For teaching math skills, situated learning could encompass settings "ranging from running a bank or shopping in a grocery store to inventing new theorems or finding new proofs. That is, situated learning can incorporate situations from everyday life to the most theoretical endeavors".

Collins cites several benefits for placing instruction within problem-solving contexts:

— Learners learn to apply their knowledge under appropriate conditions.

— Problem-solving situations foster invention and creativity.

— Learners come to see the implications of new knowledge. A common problem inherent in classroom learning is the question of relevance: "How does this relate to my life and goals?" When knowledge is acquired in the context of solving a meaningful problem, the question of relevance is at least partly answered.

— Knowledge is stored in ways that make it accessible when solving problems. People tend to retrieve knowledge more easily when they return to the setting of its acquisition. Knowledge learned while solving problems gets encoded in a way that can be accessed again in similar problem-solving situations.

3. *Modeling and explaining*: Show how a process unfolds and tell reasons why it happens that way. Collins cites two kinds of modeling: modeling of processes observed in the world and modeling of expert performance, including covert cognitive processes. Computers can be used to aid in the modeling of these

processes. Collins stresses the importance of integrating both the demonstration and the explanation during instruction. Learners need access to explanations as they observe details of the modeled performance. Computers are particularly good at modeling covert processes that otherwise would be difficult to observe. Collins suggests that truly modeling competent performance, including the false starts, dead ends, and backup strategies, can help learners more quickly adopt the tacit forms of knowledge alluded to above in the section on content. Teachers in this way are seen as "intelligent novices". By seeing both process modeling and accompanying explanations, students can develop "conditionalized" knowledge, that is, knowledge about when and where knowledge should be used to solve a variety of problems.

4. *Coaching:* Observe students as they try to complete tasks and provide hints and helps when needed. Intelligent tutoring systems sometimes embody sophisticated coaching systems that model the learner's progress and provide hints and support as practice activities increase in difficulty. The same principles of coaching can be implemented in a variety of settings. Bransford and Vye identify several characteristics of effective coaches:

   — Coaches need to monitor learners' performance to prevent their getting too far off base, but leaving enough room to allow for a real sense of exploration and problem solving.

   — Coaches help learners reflect on their performance and compare it to others'.

- Coaches use problem-solving exercises to assess learners' knowledge states. Misconceptions and buggy strategies can be identified in the context of solving problems.
- Coaches use problem-solving exercises to create the "teachable moment."

5. *Articulation*: Have students think about their actions and give reasons for their decisions and strategies, thus making their tacit knowledge more explicit. Think-aloud protocols are one example of articulation. Collins cites the benefits of added insight and the ability to compare knowledge across contexts. If learners' tacit knowledge is brought to light, that knowledge can be recruited to solve other problems.

6. *Reflection*: Have students look back over their efforts to complete a task and analyze their own performance. Reflection is like articulation, except it is pointed backwards to past tasks. Analyzing past performance efforts can also influence strategic goal-setting and intentional learning. Collins and Brown suggest four kinds or levels of reflection:

- Imitation occurs when a batting coach demonstrates a proper swing, contrasting it with your swing·
- Replay occurs when the coach videotapes your swing and plays it back, critiquing and comparing it to the swing of an expert;
- Abstracted replay might occur by tracing an expert's movements of key body parts such as elbows, wrists, hips, and knees, and comparing those movement to your movements;

— Spatial reification would take the tracings of body parts and plot them moving through space.

7. *Exploration:* Encourage students to try out different strategies and hypotheses and observe their effects. Collins caims that through exploration, students learn how to set achievable goals and to manage the pursuit of those goals. They learn to set and try out hypotheses, and to seek knowledge independently. Real-world exploration is always an attractive option; however, constraints of cost, time, and safety sometimes prohibit instruction in realistic settings. Simulations are one way to allow exploration; hypermedia structures also allow exploration of information.

8. *Sequence*: Present instruction in an ordering from simple to complex, with increasing diversity, and global before local skills.

   — *Increasing complexity*. Collins et al. point to two methods for helping learners deal with increasing complexity. First, instruction should take steps to control the complexity of assigned tasks. They cite Lave's study of tailoring apprenticeships: apprentices first learn to sew drawers, which have straight lines, few pieces of material, and no special features like zippers or pockets. They progress to more complex garments over a period of time. The second method for controlling complexity is through scaffolding. Here the cases or content remains complex, but the instructor provides the needed scaffolding for initial performances and gradually fades that support.

   — Increasing diversity refers to the variety in examples and practice contexts.

— Global before local skills refers to helping learners acquire a mental model of the problem space at very early stages of learning. Even though learners are not engaged in full problem solving, through modeling and helping on parts of the task (scaffolding), they can understand the goals of the activity and the way various strategies relate to the problem's solution. Once they have a clear "conceptual map" of the activity, they can proceed to developing specific skills.

The three teaching models presented below illustrate various features of the cognitive apprenticeship model. The first two are computer-based environments: Sherlock and goal-based scenarios. The third model is the problem-based learning environment developed by medical educators at the University of Illinois. All three models build instruction around problems or cases that are faithful to real-life situations, within which learners learn the details of a subject matter.

Goal-based Teaching

Roger Schank and colleagues at the Institute for the Learning Sciences have developed an architecture for the design of learn-by-doing courses and simulations. Goal-based scenarios constitute an alternative to traditional intelligent tutoring systems (ITS) that combine elements of simulation, case-based reasoning, and traditional ITS modeling techniques. Riesbeck (in press) describes the concept of a goal-based scenario :

> In a [goal-based scenario], a student is given a role to play, e.g., owner of a trucking company or chief scientist at a nuclear research installation, and interesting problems to

> solve or goals to achieve. The role and problems should be of real interest to the student, e.g., feeding the world, getting rich, or flying a rocket to the moon, not artificial word problems....

The student engages in a simulation in order to solve the defined problem or achieve the goal. Typically the student interacts with simulated agents and objects within a simulated environment.

Problem-based Learning

Intelligent tutoring systems rely on extensive and sophisticated cognitive task analysis to develop expert and student models; moreover, they are usually designed for individual learners. They tend to address well-structured problems in well-structured domains and build on a broad base of content knowledge. Problem-based learning (PBL) fills a different need, addressing ill-structured problems and/or ill-structured domains. Koschmann, Myers, Feltovich, and Barrows distinguished between an ill-structured domain, "in which no single concept, or even a small number of conceptual elements, is sufficient for capturing the workings of a typical instance of knowledge application", and an ill-structured problem. According to Korschman et al., ill-structured problems have the following characteristics:

— defining the problem requires more information than is initially available;

— the nature of the problem unfolds over time;

— there is no single, right way to get that information;

— as new information is obtained, the problem changes;

— decisions must be made in the absence of definitive knowledge; and

— there may never be certainty about having made the right decision.

Problem-based learning integrates the learning of content and skills, utilizes a collaborative environment, and emphasizes "learning to learn" (as opposed to case-based "learn by doing") by placing most of the responsibility for learning on the learner rather than providing a sophisticated pre-designed instructional system.

The PBL model has been implemented in several areas of higher education, including medicine, business, education, architecture, law, engineering, and social work, as well as in high school. However, the best known applications of PBL are in medical schools, where it was developed in the 1950's, and whose graduates face particularly ill-structured problems in an ill-structured and ever-expanding domain that requires life-long learning skills.

A tutor facilitates students' negotiation of five recursive stages of the problem-based methodology :

1. Problem formulation. Students isolate important facts from their rich context, identify the problem, and generate hypotheses.

2. Self-directed learning. Group members identify and address information needed to evaluate hypotheses. This list of needed information sets the learning agenda. For example, they might research basic biological mechanisms that might underlie a patient's problems, question or "examine" the patient, review results of tests they "order," and consult with the medical faculty.

3. Problem re-examination. Group members bring to bear their findings from their self-directed learning activities--adding, deleting or revising hypotheses as warranted.

4. Abstraction. This is an articulation process during which members compare and contrast cases, forming cognitive connections to increase the utility of the knowledge gained in specific contexts.

5. Reflection. At this point the group debriefs the experience and identifies areas for improvement in their learning processes.

The role of the tutor, according to Barrows, is critical to "the success of any educational method aimed at 1) developing students' thinking or reasoning skills (problem solving, metacognition, critical thinking) as they learn, and 2) helping them to become independent, self-directed learners...". The tutor must not provide mini-lectures or suggest solutions but help each member of the group internalize effective metacognitive strategies by monitoring, modeling, coaching, and fading.

8

Persuasive Communication

Although the thought of speaking before an audience fills many with feelings of dread, a public speaking opportunity, if well-planned and practiced, can be a memorable and pleasurable event for both the speaker and the audience. The purpose of communication is to transmit a message about our experiences or perceptions and to express our point of view about those experiences and perceptions. A speaker attempts to aid the audience in understanding the meaning of the message through the use of verbal and nonverbal communication. Language and words are symbolic they represent ideas and things and are the verbal tools the speaker uses to convey the true message the meaning of the words to the audience. The speaker also uses nonverbal tools attitude, actions, and appearance to share the meaning with the audience. An inspired presentation leaves the audience imbued with a real understanding of the meaning of the speaker's message, not merely superficial comprehension of the words used.

Fundamentals of Communication

Communication is a complex process, but a communication system is often categorized into six main components. The six components and their public speaking analogs are:

Transmitter:	Speaker
Channels:	Senses: speech, hearing, seeing, etc.
Message:	Speaker's topic
Receiver:	Audience
Noise:	Internal and external factors that affect message reception by audience: e.g., daydreaming, traffic noise, etc.
Feedback:	Audience reaction

Of the six components listed, the speaker has immediate control over only three: self, the methods of communication chosen, and the message itself. The speaker can influence, but not control, the last three components: the audience, distractions, and audience response. It is the speaker's role to focus attention on the audience to enhance the probability of the receipt of the message. This is done by selecting the type of communication pertinent to the message, establishing a point-of-view, and communicating its meaning to the audience. To be effective, the speaker must consciously choose not only the subject matter of the presentation, but the personal impression being made and the rhetorical tools being used. The speaker must assess his or her audience and decide how best to reach them both verbally and nonverbally.

Rhetorical Choices

Verbal Communication

Although in this section, verbal communication has been split into two major categories, persuasive and informative, in truth, all presentations have a persuasive aspect. A presentation involves motivating listeners to accept a new idea, alter an existing opinion, or act on a given premise . This is true whether the presentation is describing a recent scientific advance or a political agenda. Therefore, in both persuasive and informative speech, the speaker is asking the audience to do something whether it be accepting a scientific fact or addressing a social issue.

Persuasive Speech

Persuasive speech is used to influence both individuals and groups to accept a particular position or belief. Persuasive speech requires a clear understanding of the audience and an intense listener focus. According to Flack and Rasberry, using the problem-solution organizational pattern, the speaker must take the audience through five stages of understanding in a persuasive speech:

1) awareness of the problem,
2) understanding the problem,
3) understanding the proposed solution,
4) visualization of the effects of the proposed solution, and
5) understanding how they, the audience, must act.

The awareness stage of the persuasive speech is an introduction to the nature of the problem or situation. Audience understanding of the problem requires a concise problem statement from the speaker's point of view. It is important at this stage to show the relevancy of the problem to the audience: how the problem can or is affecting the audience. The speaker then describes the proposed solution or solutions to the problem and guides the audience into imagining how the proposed solution will be beneficial to them. Finally, the speaker enlists the audience's aid in implementing the proposed solution by indicating what actions, individually and collectively, must be taken.

Informative Speech

Informative speech is the workhorse of academia and business. The goal of informative speech is to transmit information of a factual nature: the syntax of a foreign language, the physiology of the kidney, or the sales record of a company. The topics of informative speech can often be organized by chronological or system approaches and therefore may be more easily developed than persuasive arguments. However, informative speech is often viewed as dry or boring; therefore, a speaker must be creative in using multi-sense learning techniques to maintain audience interest and engender curiosity.

Non-verbal Communication

Contrary to intuition, the brunt of the impact of a speaker's presentation is through nonverbal communication; it has been estimated that the meaning received by the audience is derived from approximately 1/3 verbal reception and 2/3 nonverbal reception. When the verbal and nonverbal messages are contradictory, most people will believe the nonverbal message they are receiving, not the verbal one. Hence, the nonverbal messages, conscious or unconscious, that are being sent by the speaker through appearance, attitude, gesture, and dress, are crucial to the communication of ideas. In addition, the speaker's ability to read the audience and change speaking strategies accordingly will also impact the effectiveness of the transmission of the message.

Appearance

The nature of your speaking environment often dictates how you will appear. For instance, if you were to speak at a formal dinner, it would be assumed that you would appear in formal dress: to do otherwise, may cause the audience to be affronted or, at least, confused. Some things to consider about your appearance:

— *Plan how you will appear.* Think carefully about what message your appearance and attire will convey to your audience: will your appearance enhance the transmission of your ideas or distract the audience from your message?

— *You are the speaker*: you need to be seen. Evaluate anything that might make you "invisible." For instance, if your long hair falls over your face when you are switching overheads (you will note this during your practice sessions), consider tying it back. People will be able to see your face, and you will not be distracted by having to push your hair out of your face.

— *Posture is important in conveying an assured presence*: stand up straight, feet approximately shoulder width apart, weight evenly distributed on both feet, and hands relaxed at your sides. Avoid slumping to one side by resting on one leg; it may seem comfortable, but it looks sloppy.

Stage Fright and Other Hurdles

Everyone gets stage fright. Some people might call it by a different name anticipatory excitement, perhaps but everyone feels excited and keyed up before a performance. Use these feelings to your advantage instead of being frightened that you might make a poor impression, be excited because you have a forum to present your ideas, you have prepared well, and you wish to present well these are all good things!

Remember, too, that your audience both wants and expects you to succeed. Few people go to a presentation hoping to have a bad time. The audience is attending your presentation with the expectation of being informed about a topic by a knowledgeable, enthusiastic speaker you!

1. *Making Friends with the Audience*: When you begin to speak, you have entered into a relationship with your audience, and your calm demeanor helps them in a number or ways:

   — A calm and confident attitude puts the audience at ease. A relaxed audience is usually more attentive and open to new ideas.

   — Extending courtesy (e.g., thanking the audience for the opportunity to speak, thanking the moderator for an introduction, tactfully handling interruptions, etc.) shows an awareness of others and establishes the speaker as a caring person.

   — Although not applicable with all topics, a cheerful and humorous attitude engages the audience and gives the audience a sense of accessibility to the speaker.

2. *Making Disasters Work for You:* Understanding the importance of having a calm attitude and having a calm attitude are two different things, however. How can you achieve a calm attitude when your knees are knocking and your palms are sweating? Act confident, even if you don't feel confident. Here are some ideas:

— Assume a power stance: feet shoulder width apart, weight evenly distributed.

— Breathe evenly from your stomach at a normal rate and depth.

— If your hands are shaking badly and you can avoid manipulating objects until the shakiness subsides, do so. If not, focus on your topic and not on your hands eventually the tremors will stop.

— If you really feel you are losing control, drop something drop the pointer, for instance. As you are bending down to retrieve it, collect your thoughts, center yourself on your topic, remember why you are there. As you stand back up, smile and make a joke "That was a refreshing break!" and continue.

— Have a sense of humor. The worst that can happen is that you do a poor job presenting your material or look extremely nervous doing it. Most people are empathetic to a nervous speaker, and if they are not, use the episode as an opportunity to build your tolerance for less than perfect performances and as learning experience.

— Practice, practice, practice prior to your presentation. Your best tool for combating nervousness is knowing your material.

Using Your Voice Effectively to Reach Your Audience

Your vocal quality and body language are key elements in presenting your message. Speak at a normal, conversational rate, and don't be concerned about using your normal hand gestures. Since you are attempting to communicate with a larger number of people than you would in a simple conversation, you will have to enhance your normal speech:

use more volume, more vocal variety, and more emphasis. As you get more experienced, you may be willing to try more theatrical, flamboyant uses of voice and gesture.Speak from the diaphragm and not from the throat. Your voice will carry better, and you are less likely to suffer from a quavering voice.

— Voice modulation is important. Avoid speaking in a monotone; use your normal conversational inflection.

— Speak at moderate speed, and enunciate clearly.

— Make sure you know the correct pronunciation of all terms and proper names in your presentation.

— Using hand gestures for emphasis during your talk can be very effective as long as they are not too wild or over-practiced. Ask for opinions from your test audience.

— It is perfectly acceptable to pause at points during your presentation; you do not have to speak continuously. Do not let brief silences rattle you. Determine appropriate "stopping points," and build pauses into the body of the presentation. Appropriately placed pauses can be quite dramatic and effective in getting the audience's attention.

— Watch for those infamous verbal pause fillers: "you know," "um," "well," and "okay?" If you use these words, you will have to train yourself to refrain from using them by being hyper-attentive to them for a few presentations; with practice, you will stop using them. You can also solicit help on breaking these habits from friends.

— Avoid the use of slang, indeterminate language, and colloquialisms in presentations. The exception to this is the "humorous aside"; however, make sure that your audience has a sense of humor before you try this.

— Do not read your presentation. Make a commitment to extemporaneous delivery. You can make your points more efficiently and effectively by speaking directly to your audience and eliciting their natural empathy.

Using Audience Feedback

In order to get and use feedback from the audience, you have to survey the members of the audience as you are speaking. It is a natural tendency, especially when you are nervous, to focus on one or two audience members as you are speaking especially if those one or two are nodding their heads in agreement. However, as the speaker, it is usually your intent to reach as many members of the audience with your message as possible. In order to do this, you must look at various members of the audience in turn and steel yourself for the possibility of seeing looks of boredom or hostility.

Look for obvious body language cues from the audience. Do they look relaxed and attentive? Are they in open postures (arms open, hands relaxed) or closed postures (arms crossed, fists clenched)? Are they watching you or looking out the window? Are they eating lunch, reading the newspaper, or even sleeping?

Do they appear confused? Often audience members will start to quietly discuss a point with each other if they are confused, will put their hand to their mouth, or tentatively raise their hands. If you observe these situations, feel free to stop and ask, "Is there a point that you would like me to explain further?"

If the nonverbal cues you are receiving from the audience indicate to you that you are not getting your message across, you'll have to be creative and modify your behavior to elicit positive audience response. For instance, you might change the modulation of your voice, use a different argument or piece of evidence to support your premise, use more open-handed gestures, or ask a question, i.e. change the format.

Do not take negative audience responses too personally, especially if only one or two people are eliciting them. Their apparent discomfort may have nothing to do with your presentation.

If an audience is responding negatively to your presentation, look at it as an opportunity to try new speaking ploys to get the presentation back on track or as an opportunity to reassess your speaking techniques.

Preparation

Setting Priorities

A presentation can be considered a form of formalized conversation. In order for you to get your point across to your audience, you must have a clear picture of the nature of your audience and its relationship to your topic. To transmit your message efficiently, you must have a listener or audience focus. What is the audience's attitude toward the topic? What is the relevancy of this topic to the audience? What is the state of audience's current knowledge of the topic? Is the audience homogeneous or heterogeneous in terms of attitude and knowledge, and how will this impact the receipt of your message? Is there only one opportunity to speak in front of this audience or will there be multiple opportunities? These are the types of questions you must ask yourself when you are organizing and developing your talk.

The essence of organizing an idea is actually very simple:

— Make a point.

— Explain it.

— Support it.

— Conclude it.

Organizing a presentation then becomes a matter of developing connections between the ideas that you have already organized.

Organizing the Main Ideas into a Coherent Presentation

In order for you to speak effectively, it is imperative that you know your topic well or can know it well by the time the presentation is to take place. Often the subject matter is dictated by the nature of your discipline or by a syllabus. As the speaker, your role is:

— to clarify the purpose, goal, or thesis of your talk, and

— to make rhetorical choices that maximize the communication of your purpose, goal, or thesis to your audience.

The most effective way to ensure that you know your topic well is by developing a thesis statement: a single simple statement that clearly and concisely states what you wish to accomplish with your presentation. Developing a thesis statement necessarily involves a narrowing of the focus of your original subject area, and this narrowing of focus should always be performed with your goals for the presentation and your knowledge of the audience in mind.

Clarify the purpose, goal, or thesis of your talk.

— Have the focus of your talk so clear that you can recite it.

— Know the point of your talk: what's the big picture?

— Why should the audience be interested in this topic?

— Limit yourself to relatively few main ideas (two to five).

— Fully develop these few main points.

— Make rhetorical choices that maximize the communication of your purpose, goal, or thesis to your audience.

— Use an organizational pattern that helps the audience follow and predict where you are headed with your topic. Develop an outline based on your thesis statement. A number of different types of outlines can be used: single word, key phrase, or complete sentence. When you are developing your outline, you should think about the type of orgaqnizational pattern most effective for your presentation. Common organizational patterns that are often used include ·

  — *Causal*: Enumerating cause and effect relationships.

  — Chronological: Sequential ordering of material.

  — *Mind map*: Using the central point of the talk as the origin in the development of a radiant, associative pattern of ideas

- *Pro and con*: Arguing the positive and negative aspects of an issue or problem.
- *Problem-solution*: Posing a problem and offering a solution.
- *Procedural:* Providing a logical ordering of the steps required to accomplish some task.
- *Spatial*: Ordering material to describe the physical arrange- ment or relationship of areas, places, or things.
- *System:* Describing the relationship of interacting, interre- lating, or interdependent parts of a collective whole.
- *Topical*: Using the topic itself to provide the organizational structure.

— Use a wide variety of supplemental material to develop your ideas.

— If your topic is complicated, consider how you can logically divide the talk into sections (or "chunks") consisting of rela- tively few points. Pay particular attention to how you are going to establish links between sections to preserve the continuity of the talk as a whole.

— Develop an introduction that sparks the audience's curiosity and gives them a reason to listen why is this topic important to them?

— Develop a conclusion that summarizes the main points that you have presented. Consider how the conclusion can be related back to the introduction bring the audience full circle.

Supporting Evidence

Both facts and opinions are used to support arguments; the selection of the mix between fact and opinion depends on what your intent is. Research has indicated that facts alone will not alter an audience's opinions; therefore, the evidence used to support a particular argument must be selected with the intended audience's current informational and belief state in mind. Evidence that is consistent with the audience's current beliefs is more likely to be accepted, particularly if the sources of that evidence are also acceptable to the audience. The evidence selected must also be understandable to the audience: use of extremely complicated or technical evidence can bore or even anger an audience. If the use of complicated evidence is necessary, the evidence must be explained carefully, and its relevance to your arguments clearly defined.

The major types of supporting evidence commonly used include:

— *Analogies*: Statements that infer a similarity between two concepts or things, usually not obviously viewed as related.

— *Anecdotes*: Short descriptions or narratives used for dramatic impact.

— *Comparisons*: Statements showing how two things relate to one another.

— *Contrasts*: Statements showing how two things differ from one another.

— *Definitions*: Statements giving the meaning of a word.

— *Examples/Illustrations*: Detailed narratives used to clarify general ideas.

- *Statistics:* Quantifications used to clarify a point, to substantiate a point, or to make an idea concrete.
- *Testimony*: Statements made by someone other than the speaker.

Some considerations when selecting supporting evidence are as follows. When using analogies, comparisons, and contrasts, you have to make sure the audience is familiar with at least one of the phenomena you are describing or your point will be lost. Definitions must be clear and concise and stated in a language easily understandable to the audience. Examples and illustrations must be carefully selected to support your points; ambiguity or illogic in your examples will hinder their usefulness. Statistics are often viewed as strong supporting evidence, but if they are overused, they can make a presentation seem boring to the audience. Testimony must be carefully selected with the audience in mind: if the audience doubts the credibility, veracity, or verifiability of the testimony, its effectiveness will be undermined.

Introductions and Conclusions

It may seem odd to place introductions and conclusions at the end of the sections on topic development, but it is after your topic is fully developed that you can see most clearly what the best way to introduce the topic is, as well as the best way to conclude it. Once you have developed your thesis statement, outlined your topic using a suitable organizational pattern, and selected your evidence, you can take a hard look at the structure of your introduction and conclusion. Your introduction should be developed to accomplish three things: establish a relationship between you and your audience, excite audience interest in your topic, and preview what you will be discussing in your presentation. You may use any type of introduction that is appropriate to your audience: use quotations, rhetorical questions, or humor. Your conclusion should accomplish two things: summarize the major points covered in the body of the presentation (post-organizing) and provide a sense of closure. One effective method for providing a sense of closure is by having the conclusion refer back to the introduction.

Audiovisual Aids

Audiovisuals aids are just that aids they should be selected to enhance the transmission of your message, not serve as either a substitute for you, the speaker, or as a smoke screen for a poorly planned presentation.

Merits of Audiovisual Aids

The benefits of carefully selected and prepared audiovisual aids are many:

— they allow multi-sense learning to take place,

— they can be used to introduce new topics and summarize ideas, and

— they can be used to clarify complex or multifaceted ideas.

Demerits of Audiovisual Aids

The drawbacks of audiovisual aids may not be as obvious:

— they can be boring and overused,

— they can be difficult to coordinate into a presentation both temporaily and technically,

— they can be time-consuming to construct, and

— they can give the speaker a false sense of mastery of his/her topic

Choosing the Audiovisual Aid

Prior to selecting an audiovisual aid, the speaker should consider the following questions:

— How will this aid enhance and support the points I intend to make in my presentation?

— How much preparation time is required for this technique?

— Is the necessary equipment available at the site? How do I make arrangements to have the equipment in place?

— Making Sure That the Selected Audiovisual Aid Will Convey the Topic Effectively.

Once you've decided on an audiovisual technique, you should:

— Make sure all visual aids are readable and accurate.

— Practice with your visual aids until your speech runs smoothly with the visual aids incorporated.

— Develop a contingency plan in the event the worst happens, i.e. an equipment malfunction occurs.

— Present only one main idea per overhead, slide, or flip chart.

— Use strong and carefully thought out transitions when using audiovisual aids.

Boardwork

Effective use of a chalkboard or whiteboard is not an easy task when speaking to an audience for an number of reasons. You must not only remember what you are about to say, you must spell correctly, write clearly, and draw organized visual aids all while turned away from your audience, thereby limiting your sense of audience feedback. For these reasons, boardwork must be carefully planned in advance.

— Plan ahead on how you will use the space on the blackboard. Use large, dark letters. Use the board from left to right. Underline or box items for emphasis as necessary.

— Use large, dark block lettering in preference to cursive writing.

— Use key words and phrases instead of complete sentences.

— Consider using colored chalk for clarity and emphasis.

— Avoid writing on the lower 1/3 of the board; usually people at the back will not be able to see what you have written because other people's heads will be in the way.

— Even if your talk is centered around overheads, be prepared to use the board. Often, boardwork is necessary during the question and answer period.

— If you need to erase, use an eraser, not your hand. You will look more in control, and you do not run the risk of ending up with chalk all over your clothes.

Flip charts

Flip charts are used more frequently in business settings than in academia, but they are an attractive alternative to boardwork in that they can be prepared in advance, are inexpensive, can be reused, and do not involve as much disruption of speaker-audience interaction as boardwork.

— Put only one main idea per chart.

— Try to put no more than 5 to 7 lines per chart.

— Use large block letters; consider the use of color for emphasis or organization.

— If necessary, you can lightly pencil in notes to yourself on the charts; however, do not obviously read these during your presentation it looks unprofessional.

— Consider attaching tabs for easier turning of the chart pages.

— Show charts only when they apply; the audience should be paying attention to you, not reading ahead on the next chart.

— Turn and talk to the chart when referring to it; increase the volume of your voice and watch your diction at any point that you are turned away from the audience.

— Watch where you are standing; make sure you are not obstructing the audience's view of the chart. Also, make sure the chart is placed high enough on its easel or stand so that persons in the back of the room have a clear view.

Overheads

Overheads are a frequently used audiovisual aid in both academia and industry. They are easy to prepare, inexpensive, and reusable. If you plan to discuss a topic to more than one audience, consider placing your most often used overheads in cardboard frames to protect them during repeated use.

— Remember that your presentation is an oral presentation not a written one. Your overheads should contain succinct phrases containing the key points that you want your audience to understand. Do not read your overheads to the audience. Your job is to verbally elaborate and defend the point of view that you are positing. Visually, you want your overheads to be easy to read and understand. Do not put too much information on each one.

— To estimate the number of overheads required for a talk, use the rule-of-thumb of 2-3 minutes per overhead, excluding the title overhead. For example, 10-15 overheads will be required for a 30-minute talk.

— Watch your margins when preparing overheads. Parts of the overhead may be cut off if the projector area is too small.

— Never put anything on an overhead that you are unwilling or unable to discuss. In the same vein, never put up an overhead, look at it, and say, "I'm not going to discuss this." If you are not going to talk about it, do not put it up!

— If you are considering using color, think carefully about why you are using it: are you color-coding items to make them more understandable to the audience or do you just think the colors look nice? There is a difference.

— Consider using "road-map" overheads, i.e. an overhead at the beginning of the talk that summarizes what topics will be covered and in what order. In the same vein, if your talk is divided into sections, consider using summary overheads that review the main points of each section.

— Use a final summary overhead that details the conclusions that you have drawn from your work.

— Do not hover by the projector; move and act naturally.

— Face the audience and speak directly to them. If you want to point to something on the overhead, use a pen, pencil, or other pointed object and point to the overhead, not to the screen.

— When not referring to an overhead, turn the projector off. This keeps the audience focused on you and removes the distraction of a bright, white blank screen.

— Try writing your notes on the paper photocopy of your overheads. In this way, your notes come up with each overhead.

— Be sure to credit your sources on your overheads; the audience should be able to easily distinguish between your work and that of others.

— After you have made your main overheads, make additional overheads in anticipation of any points that you feel may need further explanation; you will look well-prepared if questions arise, and you will feel more confident.

— If presenting your research or the work of a team effort, do not forget your etiquette overhead: thanks to your colleagues, advisor, research collaborators, post-doctoral students, other graduate students, research funding agencies, etc.

Slides

Slides are an attractive alternative for presentations that you plan to repeat for multiple audiences or for forums where slide presentations are expected, e.g. technical conferences, fine art presentations, or business presentations. Slides are more expensive financially and temporally to produce so you should allow yourself plenty of development time if you chose this audiovisual option.

— Keep in mind that the audience will be unable to use visual cues to aid in their auditory understanding when you are speaking in a darkened room; therefore, speak about twice as loudly as you normally would when giving a presentation.

— If you are using a pointer, hold it in the hand that is closest to the screen: in this way, when you point to the screen, you will be facing the audience and will not have to reach across your body to point at something.

— Take your time and describe each image or slide slowly. This is especially important when slides are being used in a classroom situation, and students are attempting to take notes.

— Decide how many images you can reasonably explain in the time period allotted, assuming that you will need approximately 3 minutes per slide or image for descriptive purposes.

— If the slide is of a physical object, give the audience an idea of the size of the actual object they are viewing.

— Develop a slide list for your presentation, both for yourself, and if the presentation is for the classroom, as a study aid for the students.

Computer graphics

Many graphics programs are available for the production of overheads and slides. Your departmental computer coordinator or the Computer Information Services (CIS) can help you decide on an application and tell you whether it is currently supported by the CIS. For instance, slide shows can be created using Macintosh's Power Point or IBM's Word Perfect Presentation for Windows.

Microphone

Using a microphone may seem uncomfortable for you the first few times that you use one: everyone remembers seeing a presentation in which the microphone failed to work, began squawking loudly, or continued to droop at the lectern like a wilted flower no matter how many times the frustrated speaker attempted to readjust it. Here are some tips on microphone use adapted from Rafe:

— If you are using a clip-on microphone, it should be place about midway on your breastbone. Rafe recommends using the hand-span technique: while looking straight ahead, put your thumb on your chin, then spread your fingers downward toward your feet. Place the microphone at the tip of your little finger.

— If you are using a microphone attached to a podium, check for the proper placement of the microphone prior to your presentation. Make sure that you know how to adjust it in the event that you must follow a speaker who has adjusted it to suit his/her needs.

— Check the audio level prior to your presentation. Introduce yourself or perform part of your introduction so you can hear how your voice is going to sound when you are delivering your talk.

— If the microphone begins screeching loudly, check to make sure that you are not standing in front of a speaker and causing feedback. If you or the technician (if available) cannot correct the problem quickly, turn the system off, and, if practical, ask the audience to move closer and continue your presentation.

— If the microphone goes dead, check to see if it was accidentally turned off or unplugged. Again, if no solution can be found quickly, continue without the microphone if practical.

Discipline specific Issues

Although there are common elements to presentations across disciplines, be aware that there may be presentation issues specific to you discipline. For instance, here are some recommendations for overheads that are specific to chemistry:

— *Rule-of-thumb for chemical structures*: do not put more than four chemical structures on an overhead. If a compound is particularly complex, it may require its own overhead.

— It is usually preferable to redraw a chemical structure than to photocopy structures out of the literature and hope they enlarge well.

— If you are presenting a graph or figure from your work, do not assume that you can photocopy it and get a good overhead. Pay particular attention to the labeling of axes and points. You may have to modify your original figure with much larger fonts in order for the labels to be readable at the back of the room.

Ask an experienced presenter in your field for advice if you have any questions about what is usual presentation practice in your discipline.

Practice Does Make Perfect

Public speaking can only be learned through direct experience; no amount of reading about it will be as effective in honing your skills as actually doing it. During your initial practice sessions, you may want to work from a fully developed written text of your talk until you are comfortable with the feel of the presentation. Having the full text of your talk written out also has the advantage of giving you a permanent record of your talk.

Once you are satisfied with the flow of your presentation, however, commit to extemporaneous delivery! Use 4 by 6 inch index cards to write key words and notes to yourself and then practice giving your talk using different phrasings to describe the meaning of your message it is the meaning, not the words, that you are trying to transmit to the audience.

Choosing Your Test Audience

There are two types of test audiences that you can select for your practice sessions, and both types have their merits. A knowledgeable test audience would be one or more persons who share your level of understanding of the topic and can make comments on the factual portion of your talk. This type of audience is very important in helping you determine the completeness and effectiveness of your coverage of a topic; however, sometimes a knowledgeable audience becomes so immersed in your topic that they are unable to give you feedback on the mechanics of your speaking skills.

A naive test audience is one comprised of non-experts in your field who can focus on how you present the material: both in terms of its logical flow and your presentation skills. If possible, a mix of both types of audience participants should be arranged for your practice sessions.

Practice in front of at least one person from your discipline (more is better) and if possible, a non-expert. Get feedback on both the organization of the material and your delivery. Listen carefully and implement changes as necessary.

The purpose of your practice talks is to give you ample opportunity to get the kinks out of your presentation. Make them as formal as possible; that is, actually present your talk do not say: "Well, first I'm going to say this and then I'll put up this overhead." Do it, do not describe it.

Use your practice session to brainstorm about the type of questions that are likely to be asked about your topic. Use your test audience to evaluate where the murky areas in your presentation are. If possible, practice in the room that you will actually be speaking in. Check your overheads and make sure that they are readable from the back of the room. When you are satisfied with the content and organization of your talk, practice, practice, practice.

Evaluating Feedback

Some members of your test audiences may be inexperienced in giving feedback. Some suggestions that you might like to share with them prior to their evaluation of your presentation are as follows:

1. *"Own" your messages.* State your reactions with "I" rather than "you" statements that generalize for all listeners. Audience reactions vary. By owning your

own reactions, you allow for the possibility of different responses.

2. *Be specific and concrete.* While it might be nice to know that someone liked my introduction, it doesn't tell me very much. Instead, one could say, for example, "I liked the concrete illustrations of the theory X." or "I liked the way you included your own background and interest in the introduction."

3. *Focus on behaviors, not on personality characteristics and judgments.* For example, say "I would have liked more eye contact" rather than "It's clear you're really not interested in us since you never look at us." Also, limit comments to behaviors that are changeable. Distracting gestures can be brought under control. Calling attention to a stutter, for example, is probably not helpful in a public setting.

4. *Distinguish between observations, inferences, and judgments.* All of these have some role in evaluation but they are quite different. Observations have to do with what we see and hear; inferences and conclusions we reach based on those observations and judgments and/or evaluative response.

   Listeners observe differently, and, more important, draw different inferences and judgments from what they see and hear. Therefore, start by reporting your observations and then explain what you inferred from them.

   Speakers can hear a great deal of feedback on observations. Inferences and judgments are more "hearable" when the observations they are based on are clear observations.

5. *Balance positive and negative comments.* Try to emphasize the positive things which the presenter might work on constructively in the future.

   When listening to feedback on your presentation, do not be overly sensitive to either the wording or the actual comments; some people may feel uncomfortable giving criticism and may not phrase their comments well. Try to understand what the test audience member is trying to say about their understanding of the message you were trying to transmit. You may be surprised what you felt was a perfectly logical argument may have been lost on your audience! Ask questions about where the audience felt they started to lose your message. Determine whether your transitions were effective.

   Although your test audience's feedback is invaluable, remember this is your presentation. Do not be intimidated into using an approach that is uncomfortable for you or inconsistent with your goals based on feedback from your test audience.

PRESENTATION

To feel comfortable prior to your presentation, it is a good idea to minimize any surprises. Therefore, get to the room in which you are presenting about one half hour early and check the following items:

— Check the audience seating arrangement. If it is unacceptable to you, modify it to suit your needs.

— Check the podium or stage. Decide how you are going to arrange your workspace to make your talk run smoothly.

— Make sure all audiovisual equipment necessary is in place and working correctly. Sound check microphones.

— If you plan to use the chalkboard at any point, make sure chalk and erasers are available.

All your practice and preparation is about to pay off! If you must introduce yourself, have a brief description of yourself, your credentials, and your interest in the topic ready. If you are being introduced by another, make sure he/she has all the pertinent information necessary to make an effective introduction.

Always remember that it is your presentation. You have worked hard to organize your material so that the audience can benefit from your expertise on a particular topic. Your presentation is the culmination of a lot of effort on your part: revel in the opportunity to communicate your ideas!

When you are introduced, smile confidently, welcome the audience to your talk, take a deep breath, and start!

Answering Questions

When preparing for your presentation, prepare for the question and answer period at the same time. When thinking about the question and answer period, you may wish to evaluate weak points in your arguments, examine subtle points that may require further explanation, or consider related material that may come up during the question and answer period. Here are some tips for handling questions:

— Embrace the notion that people are asking questions because they are curious about your topic and really want to learn something you will feel more relaxed if you are in "discussing" mode rather than "questioned-victim" mode.

— When a question is asked, repeat the question for the entire audience. This serves a number of purposes: all audience members are made aware of what issue is about to be discussed, you are made sure that you have heard the question correctly, and you are given an opportunity to start thinking of an answer.

— It is perfectly acceptable to remain silent as you formulate the answer to a question.

— If you do not understand a question, ask a question about the question or ask the questioner to rephrase question.

— If you do not know the answer to a question and can offer no educated guesses, say so (but do not apologize). If you offer to get the requested information for the questioner at a later date, follow through. If you do not know the answer but can offer a methodology for arriving at the answer, by all means do so.

— If a question is asked during your talk that is so far off-topic that it will interrupt the continuity of your presentation to address it, thank the questioner for his/her question and offer to discuss the issue with him/her after your talk.

— Keep your cool; answer questions in a calm, conversational manner even if you feel a questioner is becoming hostile or confrontational. Emphasize the positive and keep your credibility. Address the question, not the questioner.

Disasters

Even the best planned presentation can go awry sometimes because of external events such as equipment failures, last minute room changes, or even fire marshals, and sometimes because of internal events such as forgetting your place, misspeaking, making an error, or even illness. When disaster strikes, what do you do? You use Plan B.

The key for handling disasters is to have a Plan B. For instance, bearing in mind that equipment failures can occur, decide in advance how you would cope with this situation. Remember, audiovisual aids are used to enhance your presentation, but they are not equivalent to your presentation. For instance, if the overhead projector failed to function, could you still present using a blackboard? Would any material have to be left out? Is it impossible for you to present your material without your audiovisual equipment? If so, then the pre-presentation equipment check is especially crucial, and it would be beneficial to you to know the location of any spare equipment (projectors, bulbs, etc.) at your presentation site.

What about mistakes that you make during your presentation? What do you do if you suddenly find you have lost your place? One method of recovery is to repeat your last sentence, using slightly different phrasing if you prefer, as you briefly glance at your notes or overhead to reorient yourself. Often this is enough to jog your memory. What if you misspeak during your presentation? If you misspeak and it is funny and the audience laughs, laugh, too, then correct your statement and continue. Often, the best Plan B is to have a sense of humor. Maintain your positive demeanor and continue as best you can under the circumstances.

Getting Feedback from the Audience

During your practice sessions, you received feedback from the test audience that you selected. You may have modified your presentation based on their comments or you may have decided to concentrate on a new speaking technique during your presentation for instance, the effective use of pauses.

You would like and need feedback on the actual presentation. You can get two types of feedback on your actual presentation: you can arrange with someone prior to the presentation to give you feedback, telling them specifically what you would like them to look for, or you can approach persons from the audience after your presentation and get impromptu feedback from them.

Remember, if you select someone from the audience that does not know you or your topic well, they may feel uncomfortable making comments on your presentation. You will have to think carefully about what it is you would like to know and how you will phrase your questions to get the information you need.

Class Presentations by Students

Class presentations are an opportunity for students to demonstrate their understanding of a topic and to explain it to an audience. A carefully thought out speaking assignment with cogent feedback is a valuable experience for students and expands their repertoire of communication skills.

If you decide to include a speaking assignment in your course, it is best to integrate it into the course syllabus. Optional speaking assignments are often avoided by students, particularly if they do not feel they have the speaking skills necessary to perform the assignment effectively. When preparing a speaking assignment for students, here are some things to think about:

— What is the purpose of the assignment?

— What are your own goals and objectives for this assignment?

— How will you assess whether your goals and objectives have been met?

— How does this speaking assignment fit in your overall course goals?

— How will you manage the speaking assignment logistically? How will you schedule the assignment? How much time will you allot per student?

— How will you prepare the students so their presentations will be successful? In particular, how will you prepare students who have little public speaking experience or who are anxious when speaking in public?

— How will you evaluate the speaking assignment? How will you communicate your evaluation to your students?

— Will students be allowed to critique each others' presentations? What ground rules will you set for student-student evaluation?

You will probably wish to develop your own guidelines for class presentations; however, the principles outlined in the next section, Suggestions for Students, may be used as a starting point.

Suggestions for Students

Class presentations are usually fairly short (on the order of 10 minutes) so the amount of material presented must be lessened. If a longer class presentation is required for the course (on the order of 15 to 30 minutes), use the techniques and tips described in this manual to develop your presentation.

Here are some suggestions for short class presentations.

1. Your presentation should incorporate these four basic elements:

    a. State your main point clearly. Limit yourself to one main point and state it clearly and succinctly. The content of the presentation should be chosen to illustrate and support your point.

    b. Explain your main point.

    c. Support your main point with evidence from other sources.

    d. Conclude/restate your main point. Restatement of your main point helps the audience to reinforce what they have heard and remember it better.

2. Practice with others (roommates, friends, etc.).

3. State your idea in five or six different ways in order to solidify the idea in your mind and get beyond a set phrase, or a single way of expressing your idea.

4. Speak, don't read.

5. Use note cards as cues: do not read your notes. The purpose of a presentation is to give the audience your ideas about a topic, not to read out a mass of unsynthesized data.

6. Stay within the time limit.
7. Practice is critical for staying within the time assigned.
8. Do not overload a short presentation with too many extras.

9

Modern Communication Components

Two thousand four hundred years ago, the Greek philosopher Socrates realized that people understand more by answering a question, than by being told an answer. This is a very counter-intuitive idea, and it is often really hard to accept an internalize.

The reason that the Socratic method works in teaching is because a teacher through questioning can spotlight an area of knowledge, encourage students to think through the issues, establish positions, and commit to positions. It just so happens that this is exactly what the past twenty five years of cognitive science research has shown are the things that you would like someone to do when you want them to learn something.

But, there is a problem with Socratic teaching: it works well in a small group with perhaps five students. In a class of thirty, one hundred, or three hundred, most students get left out of the interaction. So, if you interact well with five students in a class of thirty, the remainder don't get the full benefit of your teaching. At the dawn of the 21st century this is unfortunate, because now we want to educate everyone, not just the elites of our societies as we did a few hundred years ago. So, it would be appropriate to use the best methods, for example, the tutorial system at Oxford and

Cambridge in England, where two to five students meet regularly with their professor ("tutor") in his/her study.

The human brain is a funny (strange) subject. One can say that it is an engineering marvel unequaled by any other system on planet earth, but this "compliment" is almost an insult to us humans. Our brain is the source of our innermost selves - the engine and soul of our species. It is almost instinctive to react when it is compared to an engineering feat, because this implies that it could be de-engineered or taken apart and understood. And, it almost certainly will, probably in the 21st century.

We already know a lot about how our minds work. In the 20th century the science of psychology has come a long way. For the first two-thirds of the time, ideas about learning were dominated by the concept of "behaviorism". Behaviorist theories of learning sought scientific, demonstrable explanations for simple behaviors. For these reasons, and since humans were considered to resemble machines, behaviorist explanations tended to be somewhat mechanical in nature. They made use of one or both of two principal classes of explanations for learning: those based on contiguity (simultaneity of stimulus and response events) and those based on the effects of behavior (reinforcement and punishment).

Some principles from behaviorist theory follow:

The following are valuable,

— Repetition

— Small, concrete, progressively sequenced tasks

— Positive and negative reinforcement

— Consistency in the use of reinforcers during the teaching-learning process

— Habits and other undesirable responses can be broken by removing the positive reinforcers connected with them.

— Immediate, consistent, and positive reinforcement increases the speed of learning.

— Once an item is learned, intermittent reinforcement will promote retention.

For many years, these concepts from behavioral theory formed the basis of most of the learning theory applied in child rearing and in classrooms. Parents and teachers still find that, in many instances, individuals do learn when provided with the appropriate blend of stimuli, rewards, negative reinforcement, and punishments. Especially with small children and simpler tasks, behavioral principles are often effective.

Eventually, however, educators began to feel that although stimulus-response does explain many human behaviors and has a legitimate place in instruction, behaviorism alone was not sufficient to explain all the phenomena observed in learning situations. The cognitive approach began to gain attention, while the behaviorist theorists went on to explore the possibilities of programmed learning for the computer age. Today, most computer-assisted instruction is solidly planted on the foundation laid by behaviorist researchers, as evidenced by the emphasis on "drill and practice" techniques.

Components of Modern Communication Education

One of the basic issues that has not yet received much attention is the end users' relation to technology in general. This question is fundamentally concerned with epistemological, ontological and axiological questions not always explicitly expressed when discussing the introduction of modern information and communication technologies (MICT) into schools. One way to classify users' relations is to point to their inner feelings of how they react to new technologies when having to face them or when getting in a position in which they will have to express their standpoint towards MICT. The following is an introductory classification which should be tested in different groups of end users, but usually it does not seem difficult to identify in the common-room, for instance, individuals representing the following categories

- Staying involuntarily or being pushed outside (dropouts)
- Being worried about or scared of MICT
- Hating or disliking any idea of having to use MICT in one's work
- Having a superficial or reluctant attitude towards MICT
- Following suit but with no authentic enthusiasm
- Imitating others (colleagues, friends) so as not to be taken for backbenchers
- At once hating and loving MICT Getting fond, perhaps little by little, of educational applications of MICT
- Pioneering, being enthusiastic about educational applications of MICT
- Acting as crackers, hackers or just leading the way

What are or what is meant by modern information and communication technologies? Historically speaking, first there was ADP (automatic data-processing), soon to be replaced by computer-based education (CBE), which was further divided into CAI (computer-assisted instruction) or CAL (computer-assisted learning) and into CMI (computer-managed instruction).

The general construct so far has been IT (information technology, sometimes technologies). In a larger perspective, IT is no longer enough, although it is still used occasionally in educational contexts as well. For instance, in the English National Curriculum, IT is said to provide a natural medium for creating, storing, retrieving and communicating information and thus being an ideal resource in language learning. Information as such is not enough; what is needed is communication. Therefore it is easily understood why a lot of researchers have started talking about communication and information technologies (les technologies de communication et d'information), abbreviated as CIT. This construct is often used in Unesco documents as well. However, in order to avoid any embarrassing connotations due to the pronunciation of that abbreviation in English, it is generally considered wiser to talk about ICT (information and communication technologies) or NICT (new information and communication technologies).

Speaking of "new" information and communication technologies is, in the final analysis, somewhat misleading, as many of the applications are based on rather old technology, i.e., on the telephone network. If "new" is used, it should be understood to imply the latest services, especially telematic and electronic. Here these technologies will be referred to as MICT (modern information and communication technologies), as it can be considered a wide enough construct to cover all up-to-date technologies and, more importantly, all pedagogical applications of earlier IT. One way of classifying MICT is given in Table 1.

The classification in Tabel 1 is meant to give a general outline on different ways of using computer applications in education. It enumerates some of the main technological developments (left column), with a few references to possible educational applications or emphases (right column). The two columns are interdependent and many components overlap as they tend to have features in common, which also means that emphases mentioned in the right column belong to several technologies on the left and vice versa. The temporal dimension covered by the left-column is fairly long, reaching up to the 21st century (e.g., ubiquitous computing). The previous classifications usually concentrate on the contemporary applications only.

Table 1. Classification of Modern Information and Communication Technologies

Computers as		"Traditional" software
stand-alone machines	▲ ▲	Computer-based training (CBT)
Audio conferencing	■ ■	Traditional distance education
Audio-graphics	■ ■	Rapid information exchange
Telefax	▼ ▼	Distance and multi-mode
Computer conferencing		education and open learning
(on-line interaction, e.g.		Individualised learning
e-mail, chat)		Simulators
Interactive CD-ROM		Electronic performance
Multimedia, hypermedia		support systems (EPSS)
Desktop video		Intelligent tutoring systems (ITS)
Video conferencing		Distance and multi-mode
Virtual reality		"full channel" communication
Virtual computing		and interaction
Ubiquitous computing		Experiential learning

As new applications keep on being launched, many educators, no doubt, whole-heartedly agree with Collis & Verwijs's statement that "we seem now to have moved from a time of comparative simplicity to one of a bewildering range of developments and terminology".

At the moment it is easy to understand that a computer which is not logged on to a communications network, is a stand-alone machine, still useful for many purposes, but with no real asset regarding a networked learning environment. From an educational point of view, it could best be described as specific to and within a given computer application. Broadly speaking, computer-based training in its conventional form can also be regarded as a general educational application.

Audio conferencing and audio-graphics rely heavily on the conventional telephone network, although cordless microphones and other equipment can also be used. Audio-graphics has made it possible to transmit graphs and pictures to remote locations, and to use an optic tablet for drawing purposes. Audio conferencing represents traditional distance education technology, still widely used.

Telefax is a special problem from an educational point of view. It certainly represents a user-friendly technology when compared to e-mail, for instance. Besides, practically all fax machines communicate with each other, which is not true of e-mail systems.

Naisbitt sees the difference between telefax and e- mail as the difference between evolutionary and revolutionary developments. Telefax is "a bridge between the old and new. Paper is slid into the fax machine much like being slid into an envelope. And the fax machine is dialed the same way the phone is. It is familiar and comfortable. Electronic mail, on the other hand, is revolutionary and does not relate to paper, only to electronics". However, Naisbitt believes that as people play more and more to e-mail's strength, it will start to gain on faxes.

Computer conferencing has widened the educational perspective by giving more open access to distance and multi-mode educational solutions. In fact, computer-mediated communication and distance education have a lot in common. In both of them, technology can take students into otherwise inaccessible environments. In distance education, the teacher's role is usually fairly active, while in computer conferencing teachers tend to become consultants or co- learners. One of the key issues to be studied further is whether some factual information or knowledge is being transferred through computer conferencing or distance education or whether more attention ought to be paid to interactional effort and process- led collaboration.

Saying that audio conferencing is largely based on listening comprehension, while computer conferencing leans back on written skills and reading comprehension is a simplification because the limits of the traditional language skills (reading, speaking, listening, writing) overlap extensively in the field of MICT. It has been pointed out elsewhere that e- mail, and computer-mediated chat in particular (e.g., communication in real time via computers), emulates the use of oral language though making use of a written mode. In fact, it is slightly surprising to notice that while oral proficiency is being underscored in many walks of life, at the same time some of the latest developments of MICT, such as cellular phones when connected to data transmission cards, have started using written messagerie (short written messages typed on the tiny screen of the phones).

From the research point of view, e-mailing and computer conferencing give ample opportunity to gather data electronically. Some of the traditional data analysis techniques, however, cannot be used when computer-mediated communication is analysed. Nordenbo points out some of the difficulties connected to these kinds of data analyses. Some analysis techniques and classifications are given in Tella.

Computer-mediated communications systems apparently offer different kinds of educational opportunities. Boyd, for instance, underlines

(i) epistemological viewpoints, connected to discursive flexibility facilitated by electronic mail systems, e.g., bi- or multidirectional (from one/many to one/many) communication vs. unidirectional communication (from one to many only), represented by mass media;

(ii) affiliative viewpoints (e.g., peer tutoring and long-term affiliations between students and their school, or among students), and

(iii) the physical flexibility offered by computer-mediated communications systems (e.g., opportunities to study in more convenient places and at more convenient times).

The main focus in CAI and CAL and in traditional computer- based software intended for educational purposes used to be on the proceduralisation of the formal elements of the target language, while in computer-mediated communication and in e-mail in particular, the computer serves not only as a learning tool but also as a tool for communication and information retrieval.

As to the position of e-mail in a broader context, Naisbitt foresees, somewhat paradoxically, that there will be a shift of emphasis towards "virtual tribes" or "electronic tribes", as e-mail is a tribe-maker. Electronics makes us more tribal at the same time it globalises us. This vision refers to the fact that e-mail and communications networks are likely to make communication more networked but laying at the same time more emphasis on telelogic communication, i.e., on small group or specifically targeted group communication.

At the moment, CD-ROMs are gaining ground in the educational sector. More and more schools are purchasing CD-ROM or CD-I players and most of the modern microcomputers already have a CD-ROM player installed when shipped to the users. Basically, a CD-ROM gives an individual learner access to an enormous amount of hypertext-based information. On the other hand, users of communications networks also access CD-ROMs without paying much attention to it. For instance, many library databases are in fact on CD-ROMs which the user accesses through communications networks.

Multimedia and hypermedia are words which mean different things to different people. Lane describes how computer, video, and audio can be combined to multimedia in an interactional model. Chou & Matsuoka talk about an integrated learning system (ILS), which is used to create a computer-based information rich constructivist learning environment, in which communications networks are made extensive use of and which involve real experts in the activities of the schools. The ambiguity of the word `multimedia' has also led to mild protestations, like in Braswell, who through a parody points out several problems connected to multimedia at school (the dollar factor; just enough to be dangerous syndrome; the Holy Grail syndrome; you don't need much time; the purpose behind repurposing).

On the other hand, it may be worth while trying to find common features between intrinsic characteristics of multi- or hypermedia and up-to-date or communicative foreign language teaching. Liu, for instance, has identified seven features common to both communicative CALL (computer-assisted language learning) and hypermedia.

EPSS is cautiously taken for a new category of educational software. Barker & Banerji define EPSS as "a custom-built interactive guidance and information support facility that is integrated into a normal working environment ... with a range of different performance support tools, each one of which will have been selected in order to aid a particular job function". One of the EPSSes could, for instance, include all sorts of tools that would help a writer browse databases on the WWW, then retrieve relevant information with key words, integrate all necessary items into a piece of writing, and then write up a complete article, to be finalised and printed out. While these kinds of tools are being built, Collis & Verwijs consider it most important to advance from a systems approach towards a human approach, which would include questions like "What are the user's activities and needs?", "How can electronic support help?"; "Balance between human and technological aspects?", etc. Finally, EPSSes should be integrated with electronic tools and environments the end user already is using for his on-going tasks.

Table 2. Paralel Features between Communicative CALL and Hypermedia

Communicative CALL	Hypermedia
• Program does not impose grammatical sequencing	• Nonsequential and nonlinear
• Program judges more to provide helpful hints	• Contextual
• Student is in control	• High level of learner control

• Student relates to subject matter in a personal way	• Learners can construct their own knowledge structure
• Student creates own learning experience	• Better accommodate learners with different styles
• Student perceives task as motivating supplement	• Multimedia aspects is a source for motivation
• Student views task as a novel activity	• Provide new experience.

Desktop video (= a PC plus a video camera on top of it) is probably going to be substituted for ordinary video conferencing systems in situations where only a few persons are interacting with one another. One of the assets of desktop video software is that communication is possible on the Internet, while ordinary videoconference systems use ISDN lines. Still, both add the visual channel to the interaction between different sender and recipient.

Not much will be said in this connection about the last categories in TABLE 1, i.e., virtual reality, virtual computing, and ubiquitous computing. What seems to characterise all these technologies is learning becoming more and more experiential. Ubiquitous computing is a certain ideal concept , which implies that by the time this ideal has come true, computing will have been wholly integrated into all educational systems. Naisbitt also argues that in the global economic network of the 21st century, information technology will drive change just as surely as manufacturing drove change in the industrial era.

Communication Channels

The problem of which channels are focused upon when discussing the question of communication is essential. In this context, three channels are often taken up, i.e., monologic communication (i.e., traditional mass media), dialogic communication (i.e., face-to-face human communication), and telelogic (or computer-mediated human) communication.

The role of communication can also be approached from other perspectives. We can for example talk about primary, secondary or tertiary communication. Primary communication can be considered as face-to-face communication, mostly in real time, for instance when having a dialogue with somebody or when delivering or listening to a speech.

Secondary communication can be represented by a number of art forms, such as theatre, while tertiary communication consists of mediated communication or, in more general terms, of computer- mediated human communication (CMHC).

Dimensionality of Communication

Another way of looking at communication is the dimensionality or directionality of communication, in which several components can be distinguished.

Basically, if communication is intended to go in one direction only, we can refer to it as one-way or monodirectional (unidirectional) communication. Two-way (bidirectional) communication emphasises the fact that both the sender and the recipient of the message can play an active role in the communication act.

Electronic mail is often considered as an example of bidirectional communication as the roles of both communicators (transceivers) are essential. A third dimensionality contains pluridirectional communication, such as computer conferencing or networking in general, in which communication is spread on several levels of communicators, either simultaneously or asynchronously, i.e., independently of time and space.

There is an eminently clear demand for clarifications as far as the classification of various combinations is concerned. Only a few anticipatory examples will be given here. An example of primary unidirectional communication would include giving an order, while an example of primary bidirectional communication could be a dialogue. In foreign language teaching, primary unidirectional communication often characterises teacher-centred lessons, during which the teacher tends to limit his use of foreign language to so-called "teacher-talk" commands. The primary target should, however, be primary bidirectional communication, in which the teacher, for instance, aims at more communicative use of the target language, relying on learners' language proficiency as much as possible.

Secondary unidirectional communication is mainly represented by traditional mass media communication, i.e., monologic communication media as they were up till the mid- and late- 1980s. Secondary bidirectional communication includes telecommunications, CD-ROMs, CD-Is, etc. Network-based communication can be depicted as secondary pluridirectional communication, which, at the moment, is growing fast.

Another way of dividing communication is through the communication channel vs. its representation. This division includes oral production (via the phone, for instance), textual production (e.g., letters, faxes), textually produced but emulating oral production (e.g., e-mail), and iconic production (e.g., graphics, audio-graphics).

Two other dimensions are worth mentioning as well: the continuum from stationary to nomadic and from isolating to networking.

Educational technology, in the traditional sense, was mainly synchronous and stationary. A language laboratory represents traditional educational technology at its best--or at its worst. However, technological progress has advanced towards more nomadic products and media, which are independent of time and place, asynchronous, transferable, light, inexpensive, and which gradually become invisible.

Traditional technology also implied isolation, to some extent at least. Language labs as well as traditional computer laboratories used to isolate learners from others while giving all of them a rigid seating order. Portable computers and laptops started to change the situation, which, thanks to cellular phones and datacards is utterly different from what it used to be.

Virtual reality is not yet here to a tangible extent but it is not difficult to grasp what thought-provoking opportunities it will give to, say, foreign language learning as soon as virtual excursions to various target countries become feasible. One step onwards will most probably be virtual computing which, according to some researchers will lead to ubiquitous computing in the 21st century.

Cost-effectiveness

"Education has by far the lowest level of investment in technology of any major sector of the economy. (Education invests an average of $ 100 per worker per year in technology, compared to an average of $ 50,000 per worker per year in many industries.)

Educational technology has also been handicapped by economic restrictions submitted to schools. The question, basically, is about how costly or how affordable certain communications media are. For the time being, communication via satellites is costly while video conferencing, especially desktop video, such as CU-SeeMe type of software, is becoming affordable at various levels of schooling. What this basically boils down to are the videophones which give full connectivity to the Internet but cost just roughly 10 % of a full-scale video conferencing system. The Kilpisjärvi Project, however, clearly demonstrates that a full video conference system using ISDN lines can also be fairly affordable.

Audio conferencing and telephony in general have been studied in quite a few countries for years now. Audio conferencing, when combined with audio-graphics, for instance, has proved a success even if in the conventional solution two telephone lines are needed.

At the most affordable end of the scale, educators have had recourse to videotapes, audiotapes, cassettes, minidiscs, etc. These represent conventional if not widely and universally available technology which few educators fight against.

Power and Responsibility

Power, authority, and responsibility--both assuming responsibility and allowing others to assume responsibility--are delicate issues in communicative media education. Power as exercised by the teacher is sometimes divided into four different categories: authoritative, autonomous, authoritarian, and abdicated power. As far as MICT are concerned, power is constantly a topical issue which should be studied carefully in various research settings.

Another way of thinking of power is the continuum from monologue to dialogue and polylogue. In order to facilitate dialogue, the teacher has to be able and willing to give up his own monologue. Dialogue will change into an authentic polylogue only if constructivist principles are respected and mutual discussion encouraged. Polylogue is basically a fundamental way of conversation and an exchange of ideas in computer conferencing, but it can be hampered if the technical or pedagogical manager of the conference occupies too much scope of the conference's virtual space. Consequently, the question can be traced back to the role of monopoly or the teacher's (the manager's authority) in comparison to authentic dipoly (two communicators' authority) or tripoly, in which several communicators respect each other's right to express themselves. In many respects, this is closely connected to the question of electronic leadership, which appears to be one of the most important factors as far as the success of an electronic conference is concerned.

Mass Communication

Most of the above factors are also linked to the question of whether communication and instruction are being individualised or oriented towards mass communication. Modern information and communication technologies give access to individualised learning tools and make it easy to organise an individualised or learner-focused learning environment which, however, takes advantage of extensive physical and conceptual networking. In the same way, dyadic forms of work are facilitated as well as small group constellations.

Telelogic communication emphasises small specialised group communication or target group communication, while traditional mass media (radio, television or the so-called electronic media in comparison to telematic media, such as e-mail, computer conferencing, WWW, gophers, Archie, FTP, etc.) aim at reaching large audiences.

The benefits of networked computers are accepted as a new starting point. Sawyer cites America 2000 in that "[b]y far the most promising benefit of networked computers for education lies in extending the network to include access to computing from the homes of teachers and students. This would address head-on one of the most difficult roadblocks to educational improvement ... Non-classroom access to a significant learning tool would be especially important in the case of disadvantaged students ... access to a personal computer in the home ... could provide a powerful alternative to entertainment television or the street. If students had home access to personal computers integrated into the curriculum and linked to the schools' library resources, they would be able to extend their classroom exposure by repeating lessons missed in class, retrying simulation-based `lab experiments,' and preparing homework using the computer for library access, word processing, drawing, music study, and computation. ... The home time available to students during each week of the school year could easily equal the time spent in the classroom. During the summer vacation, the same computer facility would be available for educational gaming, electronic mail, summer projects, and adult literacy or other training programs."

Communication/Education/Teaching

In the final analysis, the question is about the subtle differences between media communication education, communicative media education and educational media communication on one hand, and about communication as communication or communication as educational communication on the other hand, and, in the final analysis, between teaching, studying, and learning as well as about the shifts of emphasis in learning paradigms, concepts of learning and knowledge in connection with the changes in teachers', students' and schools' status

Communication, implicitly, covers everything as everything is communication per se, verbal, non-verbal or at least paralingual or extralingual. Teaching may include studying and learning, but there has been a strong shift of emphasis from teaching-based approaches towards learner-centred or learner-sponsored approaches. When speaking about open multimedia-based and networked learning environments or about virtual schools, we have to bear in mind that the word `learning' in the English language also implies studying, while in Finnish it mostly refers to the product of studying. Or perhaps we should start to underline the importance of education as an overall term; speaking of primary, secondary, adult and lifelong education may also lead us to start talking about computer-based education with a special emphasis on computer-mediated communication, which seems to cover most of the features human-to-human communication has always included. Consequently, open learning and distance education are terms whose role and significance are likely to increase in the years to come.

Significances of Graphic Communication Education

Production processes are undergoing fundamental changes brought about by the introduction of digital technologies. In fact, the digitization of the workflow is the Industrial Revolution of the twentieth century: Two hundred years ago, the graphic arts industry adopted the steam press and hot type foundry, eliminating hundreds of jobs. Today, the "digital revolution" is cutting back human resources in favor of automated processes.

Innovations adopted as a result of digitization not only include computer-to-plate and direct-to-press processes, but also digital printing. However, the new technologies have not only changed print production, but they have also expanded the realm of graphic communications to a variety of electronic media such as CD-ROM publishing and the Internet, which are capturing growing segments of the print market. However, far from limiting the job market, the increased use of digital technologies has expanded the employment opportunities of graphic communication technologists. The publishing industry reports a shortage of qualified employees, reflecting a demand for industrial technologists specializing in graphic communications and the graphic arts.

An analysis of the industry's needs suggests a redefinition of the graphic arts education to include image generation in addition to image reproduction. Furthermore, this explains that today's graphic communication includes both print and electronic media, fusing the formerly split fields of still and dynamic image generation. Finally, it is argued that the potential growth of the professional realm of graphic communications will extend only if these changes are embraced by educational institutions. Graphic communication technology curricula need to include electronic publishing and multimedia production technologies in order to fill the job niche created by the development of new media.

The digital workflow has all but extinguished most of the traditional "composing room jobs" such as compositor, layout man, proofreader, linotype-intertype operator and monotype operator. The only "survivor" is the "layout man," known today as a "graphic designer." Once exclusively concerned with image generation, graphic designers are now taking over a variety of production responsibilities in addition to the visual conceptualization of information.

Working in close relationship with printers and electronic publishers alike, designers are often in charge of preparing artwork for proper ripping, trapping and color separating. Likewise, many of the pressroom positions such as the platemaker, electrotyper, stereotyper, and photoengraver have collapsed into the electronic pre-press technician who handles all of the preprinting requisites through a computer. Moreover, it is not uncommon to find the graphic designer's and the pre-press technician's duties done by the same person. Hence, today's graphic communication professionals need to be as proficient in image generation as in graphic reproduction in order to respond to the industry's needs where automated technology is fading out numerous print positions.

However, while digitization is limiting the job market in traditionally defined graphic arts, employment opportunities in image generation are expanding. In October 1998, "TrendWatch" a monitor of changes in the graphic arts, publishing, and electronic media markets, reported that despite the fact that the pre-press industry lost 29% of the firms and 16% of the production jobs since 1990, employment in the graphic arts did not suffer. On the contrary, finding qualified employees has been one of the top concerns of printing and trade managers.

According to "TrendWatch," graphic communication technologists are joining the creative sector, an area that is growing considerably. In 1998, the number of creative establishments rose by 11.5% and the number of creative employees expanded by 12.5% in comparison to 1997. The increased production responsibilities at the creative stage of the graphic communication production and the growing demand for professionals skilled to take on such responsibilities are a direct consequence of the growing capabilities of personal workstations.

With the advent of the computer, the realms of image generation and reproduction have overlapped to form one field in which technology literacy is a primary requisite. This kind of expertise, however, is difficult to obtain and to maintain at today's pace of innovations. In the graphics industry, pre-press and electronic publishing have brought a wave of opportunities requiring skills that have not been a part of a graphic communicator's education in the past.

In 1998, the London College of Printing conducted a study analyzing the training needs of the pre-press industry. The study identified a skills gap generated by the convergence of once highly differentiated text, image origination and manipulation areas into one that allows for still and moving images to be treated within a single digital environment. While this convergence has spawned opportunities for companies to expand into new areas of operation providing alternative media services to clients, the study suggested that growth in these areas has been hampered by the need for employees with digital media skills.

Future of Graphic Communications

Multimedia-the combination of text, images, sound, and motion-has evolved into a powerful information tool. The growth of this medium is directly related to the use of personal computers and their increased media capabilities-most notably, the Internet, which is currently one of the main outlets for multimedia communication. A growing number of businesses are establishing a presence on the Internet by hosting web pages, which oftentimes allow consumers to purchase goods, but are also frequently only used as a means of contact and promotion.

For its multimedia capabilities, electronic publishing has been perceived as a threat to the print publishing market. In fact, at the beginning of the 90s, electronic publishing was predicted to replace print media entirely. Hypothetical scenarios, such as the "paperless office," described a world of electronic transfer and display of information with no need for print. However, as far as paper consumption is concerned, time has proven the opposite. While more information is being transmitted digitally, the sheer quantity of information is expanding and more of it is printed on consumers' personal laser printers.

Nevertheless, the growth of electronic media has affected the book publishing industry, where such companies as Doubleday, Putnam, and McGraw-Hill have registered major cutbacks. Although the decline in the book market is strongly related to the increased use of a variety of other media such as radio, television, movies and video, -which have competed with books for several decades, - more recently, the direct competition of the printed book is the CD-ROM.

After two decades on the market, CD-ROM publishing has proven a versatile medium that allows readers to interact and customize their access to information. The advantage of this medium lies in its capability to deliver what today's hyper-stimulated society demands: a high-capacity, dynamic, non-linear and multi-sensory medium. In fact, CD-ROMs are already being replaced by Digital Video Discs (DVDs), whose storage capacity outperforms the former at a rate of 14 to 1.

In addition, the Internet is influencing the print publishing industry by providing access to catalogs, indexes, books, magazines and other information that used to be available only in print, allowing readers to bypass the need for acquiring a published copy for themselves. An ever-increasing variety of materials has been made available on the Internet, catering to the 129 million English-speaking users estimated to access the Internet in 1999. However, with the exception of the Internet, the adoption of multimedia has been slower than expected.

In 1994, interactive media advertising spending totaled $135 million, primarily for online services and CD-ROMs, which was far lower than anticipated. In the book publishing industry, consumers were expected to turn to multimedia in lieu of printed books. However, in 1996, numerous CD-ROM publishers went out of business, cut back their title output, or merged with other companies.

Nonetheless, while the multimedia market has fallen short of its expectations, it should not be dismissed. Recent reports indicate that the demand for interactive and multimedia advertising is slowly increasing and CD-ROM publishers are revising the applications of this medium, focusing on growth markets such as children's education, reference titles, and book/disc packages. Thus, while multimedia electronic publishing has not taken over the print publishing industry, it is certainly evolving into a powerful medium.

In addition, multimedia is making its way to the corporate realm beyond sales and marketing departments. Corporations are exploring the use of multimedia training programs, interactive internal communication via Intranet servers, and CD-ROM publishing. For example, industries such as health care and airlines streamline operations with integrated voice and imaging applications. Also, the manufacturing industry uses multimedia programs such as

IBM's Paperless Manufacturing Workplace, which provides text, vector and rasterbased graphics, video, user written programs, and engineering instructions to workstations on the manufacturing plant floor. However, the major restraint in the growth of the multimedia industry is the rapid pace of technological changes, an intimidating factor that has prevented many companies from developing missioncritical multimedia systems.

For a large number of companies the need for training and constant updating is a major deterrent to make large investments in technology-based communication. In 1995, 36% of large and medium-sized businesses revealed no interest in multimedia and more than half said they were only moderately interested. A mere 2.6% of surveyed businesses were enthusiastic about incorporating multimedia technologies into their business strategies, suggesting that the continuous development of digital technologies and the subsequent need to keep up with it has prompted companies not to embrace multimedia.

In the field of graphic media production, where multimedia is being developed professionally, technological innovations pose a similar challenge. A great variety of industries and especially the publishing industry, are dependent on technology and respond to it by placing increased importance on the technological literacy of their employees. Therefore, digital media competence, coupled with knowledge of the graphic communication production processes is a highly desirable qualification.

The shortage of qualified employees experienced by the publishing industry provides evidence of a shift in the profile of graphic communication graduates sought by the industry. A new focus places increased importance on image generation and electronic publishing, in addition to print reproduction. Graphic communication specialists with this kind of expertise are in great demand not only by the graphic arts industry, but also by a variety of other companies, such as web design studios. Businesses are venturing into Internet and other multimedia marketing strategies, and are thus employing graphic communications specialists.

In addition, companies that used to outsource their printing needs are adopting desktop publishing technologies to produce business communication pieces in-house. Undoubtedly, in an age where more paper is consumed than ever before, graphic communications employment opportunities are shifting from the press to the computer, from the actual printing process to the formatting of information for electronic access.

In recent years, educational programs have started to modify their curricula in accordance with the increasing demands for graphic communication graduates with high command of digital technologies. High schools in the Los Angeles area, for example, are teaching computer animation and both the Department of Industry and Technology at the University of Pennsylvania, and Colorado State University have been hosting computer animation workshops for K-12 youth for several summers.

At the college level, graphic communications programs have also commenced to embrace new media technologies. As is usually the case with fundamental changes, the transition is slow and costly. The same factors of rapid technological change and uncertain investment value that inhibit the industry from adopting multimedia fearlessly are halting educational institutions. At the present rate, computer-related courses need to be redeveloped on a yearly basis with considerable investment not only of hardware and software, but also in terms of time and effort. One of the top centers of education for graphic arts and printing professionals, the Graphic Communication Department at California Polytechnic State University, has long offered degrees in three major areas: "Printing Management," "Design Reproduction Technology," and "Computers and Printing Technology."

In order to better reflect the recent developments in the digitization of the industry, the Computer and Printing Technology area was renamed "Electronic Publishing and Imaging" in 1997.

At the California Polytechnic, graphic communication instruction includes internet publishing, computer imaging, desktop publishing and multimedia. In addition to state-of-the-art print production facilities, California Polytechnic also features electronic pre-press, design reproduction technology and digital electronic imaging labs.

Students of this select program reportedly receive three to five job offers before graduating. Notably, California Polytechnic not only includes electronic pre-press in its curriculum, but also multimedia, blurring the limits between motionless and dynamic graphic communication.

Multimedia is the discipline that has blurred the boundaries of such areas as television, video, and animation with the graphic arts into one field: graphic communication. The transition initiated by California Polytechnic is a model to follow. Not many educational programs have made the leap towards electronic publishing and digital image generation running the risk of ill-preparing their graduates. The existing skills gap in graphic communication technologies is a market niche waiting to be filled by industrial technology programs.

TEACHING AND LEARNING WITH THE INTERNET

The communication of ideas in the industrialised world is experiencing a period of change unparalleled since the mass-production of books and the introduction of the telegraph in the nineteenth century. Current change is being driven by the apparent convergence of mass media, telecommunications and computer technologies coupled with the transition from analogue to digital coding of information. The Internet is central to this change.

Ten years ago, few could have foreseen how rapidly the Internet would spread from universities into business and then find its way into the home. The take-up in the last five years has been spectacular, not least in the Nordic countries. Here household penetration of computers passed the 50% mark in 1998 and Internet access from the home is in all cases higher than 25%. Three-quarters of Danish school children have access to a computer (usually with a CD-ROM drive and increasingly with Internet access) at home.

Note that using a computer is now as common as watching video and has overtaken reading in the last five years. Such changes are also found in other European countries. According to a recent NOP survey, 3 million UK Internet users are aged 17 or under, a 12% increase since January 1999. Remarkably, 61% of the online youths are female, compared to 19% of the 55 years and older Internet users. In the UK, boys and girls have different usage habits.

Boys use the medium to access entertainment information, and download music and software, while girls tend to use the medium more to interact with other people (chat & email). Young Internet users are often engaged in another activity while surfing: 58% listen to music, 23% watch TV, 13% listen to the radio, another 13% read a magazine. Children perceive Internet users as clever, friendly, cool, trendy and rich.

Whereas computers are widely used at work and in the home, they are less ubiquitous in schools in spite of having made their first appearance there in the late sixties. In the intervening period, educational policies regarding information and communication technologies (ICT) have moved through three major phases:

— Teaching computing as a subject

— Using multimedia computers as a learning resource within the curriculum

— Connecting computers locally within schools and classrooms and providing regional, national and international links with others.

Internet technology is central to this third phase. The global reach of the Internet has a dual nature in education; it is both an end in itself and a means to an end. It is an end in its own right when the Internet, the Information Society and economic growth are seen as inter-related phenomena. It is a means to an end when the focus is on improving the quality of teaching and learning or improving the productivity of the education system.

Complementary programmes cover in-service teacher training, equipping libraries, digitising content in libraries, museums and galleries, and public/private partnerships for the provision of digital content for lifelong learning. The key concern in such initiatives has been the physical infrastructure, getting computers into schools and getting them wired in order to provide:

1. Internet access within a school

2. E-mail access for pupils and students

3. E-mail access for teachers
4. School intranets

Once the infrastructure is in place, the investment will only bear fruit if it leads to changes in mainstream teaching and learning. This requires in-service teacher training and a framework in which suitable content can be created, maintained and distributed.

Courseware Engineering and Instruction

What is known about human learning relevant for the design of educational material? How should this knowledge be used in the context of more specific educational goals and WWW-supported learning & teaching activities? Generally speaking there are two important statements about learning and instruction:

— One learns by doing something (psychology)

— One learns by pursuing an instructional goal (education sciences)

The learning environment designer must take into account both perspectives. WWW-based courseware must not restrict itself to delivery of educational content. It must be grounded in some model of instruction and learning. Many possibilities exist and haven proven to be effective. However, each paradigm works under certain conditions in certain situations using some set of specific educational technology. For example, it can easily be argued that a good book is better than hypertext version of that book (why do people always print out things?).

Also, general rules can be formulated such as "learning without doing is pretty useless in most domains".

Consider the following questions:

— Would you take the plane if you knew that the pilot has read all the documentation about flying and successfully passed examination testing his knowledge?

— Would you take a plane if you knew that the pilot has been trained with Microsoft flight simulator? Which one do trust better?

— Would you take an Airbus if you knew that the pilot has been trained on a B-737 and has read the WWW multimedia Airbus documentation?

— If you had to teach flying an Airbus, would you take a would-be pilot and show him how to fly "hands-on"?

Some basic misconceptions about learning have to avoided: Reading or seeing does not imply much learning. Even being able to recall knowledge does not mean being able to apply knowledge. Efficiency is not measured by mastery of the exercises and tests of a courseware tool, but the mastery of the task.

Also be aware of more subtle knowledge transfer problems: Even "micro"-competencies such as operating an Airbus vs. a Boing or programming in C instead of Pascal are difficult to teach. If more abstract things like "programming" instead of just C programming have to be learned, special teaching strategies have to be used (such exercising skills in variating contexts. Lastly, the complexity of a learning environment must be adapted to the learners skills (Would you teach C as an introductory programming language)?

Courseware engineering is concerned with electronic learning environments. Such an environment is a combined system involving tasks, agents, courseware products, etc. which is aimed at supporting learning processes and in which learning takes place mostly in interaction between learners, courseware products, other tools, and to a lesser degree tutors (human or artificial). Courseware is always a combination of elements, such as:

— textual material (including textual representations)

— simulation models,

— exercises

— problems

— feedback information, etc.

Each type of courseware architecture organizes those resources in various ways. How complete are the materials supplied to the learner with respect to the information and support needed by the learner to achieve an instructional goal? Several ways of tackling this problem have been proposed.

We shall briefly introduce some ideas from (1) Instructional Design and from (2) Advanced Learning Environment Research.

Instructional Design Theory

What learning activity can we do with the Web? Here is a (short) list of different kinds of computational learning environments in use. They represetn different learning paradigms and can be classified along several axes like "Instruction - Learning", "External - Internal Control". Each are still appropriate for certain kinds of learning.

— Programmed Instruction (little step by step transfer of content)

- — Computer Assisted Instruction (Drills & Tutorials)
- — Intelligent Computer Assisted Instruction (ITS Tutorials)
- — Computer Based Learning (Simulations, Hypertext & Microworlds)
- — Intelligent Learning Environments (Microworlds + tutors, helpers, experts)
- — Cognitive Learning Support Environments (some hypertexts)
- — Knowledge Construction & Environments & Intellectual Toolkits

Now match that to those more technical items:

- — Information servers to look up information (manuals, books, expositions, bibliographies, programs, etc.)
- — Distribute educational material (texts, programs)
- — Provide curricula & guidance to lessons and exercises in hypertext format.
- — Implement collaborative work (dynamic hypertext, "News like conferencing system", co-writing)

Implement Jigsaw puzzles

- — Question & Answering, (tests, Skinner & Bloom type of learning to some extent)
- — Interface to local clients (e.g. simulations, programming environments, tutors, etc.)
- — The same thing over the web (e.g. have intelligent nodes, cf. Mallery)

The WWW, specially in conjunction with external local or server-side clients offers a lot of possibilities. But not everything can be done and it is important not to use in inappropriate learning paradigm for a given educational goal.

Integration of Hypermedia

There are 3 aspects:

— Integration into a learning environment setup: What role in learning & teaching does hypermedia have? What other tools do we need?

— Integration into a learning environment architecture: How can we make integrate hypermedia with other computational learning tools?

— Computational integration with other programs: How can we build achieve tight integration?

Courseware Engineering and the Learning Environment

In more simple and technical terms, courseware engineering is concerned with:

— transferring educational information

— organizing pedagogically optimized access to this information via an appropriate interface and structuring of the material

— implementation of instructional tactics, e.g.:

— giving examples

— multiple choice questions

— asking the student to perform a task, etc.

— telling the student what learning strategy to adopt with some material

— implementation of instructional strategies, i.e. sequencing of teaching materials

Furthermore, Courseware engineering is not everything. Courseware alone rarely constitutes the full learning environment. Authors of Instructional Material on the Web should be aware of the following:

— Teaching and learning involves a learning environment. It is not good enough to hypertextify a text or implement form-based tests. Good Web based courseware is more global in design. Not everything must be built into html or server-side scripts, but somehow instructional tactics & strategies as well as learning strategies have to be "put" upon the learner or communicated to the learner. Last, but not least he needs assistance and very often cooperation with other learners.

— Delivery of instructional text (multimedia and hypermedia) has be structured according to some pedagogical & learning strategies. If the learner has to discover everything himself - fine - but tell him so!

Use of the Web

In discussing the role of technological support in education, Sandberg identifies the components of a (technologically rich) learning environment. These components must all be there in order to optimize learning. However, they can be "implemented" in many different ways. Each component has functionalities for which we should insure:

— *teacher:* His role is provide something between loose guidance & direct instruction. It can be a human agent (present or distant) or an intelligent agent. He provides information from the curriculum to the task level.

- *monitor:* The Monitor ensures that something is learner. A role taken by either the teacher, the learner (self-control) or by some program.
- *fellow learners:* Improve the learning process (some research tries to implement artificial ones)
- *learning material:* Learning material contains what has to be learned in a very broad sense (e.g. knowing what, knowing how). It can be computational in various ways (exploratory hypertext, lesson & task oriented hypertext, simulation software, task solving environments, etc.
- *External info sources:* All kinds of information which is not directly stored in the learning material (e.g. additional material, handbooks, manuals, etc.)
- *tools:* Everything which may help the learning process other then the learning material (e.g. calculators, communication software, etc.)

Recent years have shown an explosion of interest in using computers for language teaching and learning. A decade ago, the use of computers in the language classroom was of concern only to a small number of specialists. However, with the advent of multimedia computing and the Internet, the role of computers in language instruction has now become an important issue confronting large numbers of language teachers throughout the world.

Since its emergence thirty years ago, the Internet has metamorphosed from a communications tool immune to the ravages of nuclear weapons to a narrow band infrastructure for global communication and information. Recent developments both in homes and businesses indicate that it is set to go through another step in this metamorphosis.

The first aspect is the change from narrow band to broadband access. Small businesses and homes in the United States are already being offered bandwidths of between 400 kilobit and 6.7 megabit by Internet service providers operating over digital cable, Digital Subscriber Lines (ADSL, G-lite and VDSL) over telephone wires and even via digital satellite. The take-up of services by companies such as AT&T and @home is such that at least 30% of all Internet subscribers are expected to be on a broadband connection within 5 years. If this happens in the home, broadband is sure to make itself felt in education.

For those accessing the Internet by phone or ISDN, connection charges are a significant part of the operational budget - users pay the telecommunications company for the duration of their connection. The new broadband services usually charge either a flat rate or for the amount of data received and sent. The move from dial-up access to broadband will mean that users at school and in the home can be connected round the clock. Anecdotal evidence from blocks of flats and from institutions "always on" suggests that the patterns of Internet use will change radically when there is sufficient bandwidth to receive and send audio, images and video and when users no longer need to dial-up.

The Internet Protocol (IP) governing the technicalities of changing information into packets so that they can be distributed via the Internet is also beginning to make itself felt in the convergence of digital television, mobile telephony and the Internet per se. Digital television via satellite and cable is already on the market, soon to be joined by digital terrestrial television. The first services on digital cable which allow the combination of television and the World Wide Web are already available, although no-one is certain what the final form of convergent services will take.

Countries such as the UK and Sweden have already launched digital television channels specifically for education. BBC Knowledge began services in June 1999, and the Swedish Knowledge Network is planned to commence operations by the autumn of 1999. Both have the potential of combining interactivity with attractive broadcast content in the form of enhanced or interactive television. For the less affluent in Europe, a set-top box offers a cheap and attractive alternative to Internet access from the home, albeit in the form of a more limited range of services. It is thus clear that the Internet in various guises will be found on a range of digital services, not just on narrow band Internet accessed by a computer.

A qualified guess is that subscription services and pay-per-use will gain ground as business models for these convergent interactive multimedia services and provide new opportunities for out-of-school and lifelong learning accessible to the many, not just the privileged few. When discussing business models for educational resources on the Internet, we will have to formulate strategies that allow for the metamorphosis of the Internet and the potential of IP services via digital television.

Use of Computer-assisted Language Learning (CALL)

Computers have been used for language teaching since the 1960s. This 30+ year history can be roughly divided into three main stages: behavioristic CALL, communicative CALL, and integrative CALL. Each stage corresponds to a certain level of technology as well as a certain pedagogical approach.

Behavioristic CALL, conceived in the 1950s and implemented in the 1960s and 1970s, could be considered a sub-component of the broader field of computer-assisted instruction. Informed by the behaviorist learning model, this mode of CALL featured repetitive language drills, referred to as drill-and-practice (or, pejoratively, as "drill-and-kill"). In this paradigm, especially popular in the United States, the computer was viewed as a mechanical tutor which never grew tired or judgmental and allowed students to work at an individual pace. Though behaviorist CALL eventually gravitated to the personal computer, it was first designed and implemented in the era of the mainframe. The best-known tutorial system, PLATO, ran on its own special hardware consisting of a central computer and terminals and featured extensive drills, grammatical explanations, and translation tests at various intervals.

The next stage, *communicative CALL,* emerged in the late 1970s and early 1980s, at the same time that behavioristic approaches to language teaching were being rejected at both the theoretical and pedagogical level, and when new personal computers were creating greater possibilities for individual work. Proponents of communicative CALL stressed that computer-based activities should focus more on using forms than on the forms themselves, teach grammar implicitly rather than implicitly, allow and encourage students to generate original utterances rather than just manipulate prefabricated language, and use the target language predominantly or even exclusively.

Communicative CALL corresponded to cognitive theories which stressed that learning was a process of discovery, expression, and development. Popular CALL software developed in this period included text reconstruction programs (which allowed students working alone or in groups to rearrange words and texts to discover patterns of language and meaning) and simulations (which stimulated discussion and discovery among students working in pairs or groups). For many proponents of communicative CALL, the focus was not so much on what students did with the machine, but rather what they with each other while working at the computer.

Though communicative CALL was seen as an advance over behavioristic CALL, it too began to come under criticism. By the late 1980s and early 1990s, critics pointed out that the computer was still being used in an ad hoc and disconnected fashion and thus "finds itself making a greater contribution to marginal rather than central elements" of the language learning process. This corresponded to a broader reassessment of communicative language teaching theory and practice. Many teachers were moving away from a cognitive view of communicative teaching to a more social or socio-cognitive view, which placed greater emphasis on language use in authentic social contexts. Task-based, project-based, and content-based approaches all sought to integrate learners in authentic environments, and also to integrate the various skills of language learning and use.

This led to a new perspective on technology and language learning, which has been termed *integrative CALL*, a perspective which seeks both to integrate various skills (e.g., listening, speaking, reading, and writing) and also integrate technology more fully into the language learning process. In integrative approaches, students learn to use a variety of technological tools as an ongoing process of language learning and use, rather than visiting the computer lab on a once a week basis for isolated exercises.

If the mainframe was the technology of behavioristic CALL, and the PC the technology of communicative CALL, the multimedia networked computer is the technology of integrative CALL. The multimedia networked computer—with a range of informational, communicative, and publishing tools now potentially at the fingertips of every student—provides not only the possibilities for much more integrated uses of technology, but also the imperative for such use, as learning to read, write, and communicate via computer has become an essential feature of modern life in the developed world.

Many of the changes in CALL paradigms flow from economic and social changes. The shift to global information-based economies has meant a dramatic increase in the need to deal with large amounts of information and to communicate across languages and cultures. Memorization is less important in this information-rich time than effective search strategies, and students need the ability to respond and adapt to changes rather than training in a single way to approach a task.

Teacher roles have also changed with the times. Teachers are rarely the sole source of language information in these days of global interconnectedness, and the literary corpus that may have been the basis of their foreign language training is not the only body of knowledge worth learning.

The assumption from cognitive theory is that teachers do not pour information from their store into the heads of waiting and willing students, but that students actively interpret and organize the information they are given, fitting it into prior knowledge or revising prior knowledge in the light of what they have learned. As a result of all these changes, the teacher has become a facilitator of learning rather than the font of wisdom, and will find, select, and offer information in a variety of ways on the basis of what their students must learn in order to meet diverse needs.

Having and manipulating language data in multiple media provides learners with the raw material they can use to re-create the language for themselves, using their own organizing schemes. Activities that encourage students to explore and be creators of language rather than passive recipients of it further the idea of the learner as an active participant in learning. While both teachers and learners see some utility in basic language drills, such as of irregular verb forms, repetitive practice only fits into a small part of language learning when the goal is communication in the target language.

As facilitators, teachers must in many ways know more than they would as directive givers of information. Facilitators must be aware of a variety of material available for improving students' language skill, not just one or two texts. They also need to know how to teach learners to use the material effectively. Teachers as facilitators have to be able to respond to the needs that students have, not just what has been set up ahead of time based on a curriculum developer's idea of who will be in the classroom. Teacher training is a key element to success in this more flexible language classroom, so that teachers can use multimedia and other resources effectively.

Current Practices

The three stages mentioned above do not fall into neatly contained timelines. As each new stage has emerged, previous stages continue. Current uses of computers in the language classroom correspond to all three of the paradigms mentioned above. We will begin this examination by looking at the teaching practices and research on the use of stand-alone CALL software programs. We will then analyze practices and research on the uses of the Internet in language learning and teaching.

CALLSoftware

One of the reasons that administrators buy software is with the thought of providing an integrated teaching solution—something that will

(1) provide realistic, native-speaker models of the language in a variety of media

(2) offer a language learning curriculum

(3) do a needs assessment

(4) determine the best next step for the learner and provide practice with that skill area

(5) record what the student has done, along with an evaluation

(6) be available at any hour and require no additional pay or benefits

A number of high-end packages have been designed to come as close as possible to meeting those needs in terms of English language teaching. These include CALI's *Ellis*, DynEd's *Dynamic English*, Berlitz's *English Discoveries*, Jostens' *English Language Development* and *STEPS*, and Hartley's *Project Star*. *ESL 2000* from HRB Systems incorporates software from some of these and other vendors into a comprehensive system that includes management software. What distinguishes these from many other multimedia programs is that they include a curriculum, not just distinct elements for practice.

The quality of the curriculum and its relevance to the target learners is a matter for each institution to determine, since each of the packages is designed with a somewhat different group of learners in mind. Some, like the Jostens and Hartley products, are made for a North American

English as a Second Language audience; others, such as the CALI and DynEd offerings, are geared more toward an English as a Foreign Language setting.

Another similarity in these high-cost products is their relative immutability. There is little or no provision for teacher-customized content. After all, it would be difficult to incorporate teacher-generated lessons into a fixed curriculum. Some of the programs have teacher's guides and suggest ways to incorporate the lessons into a regular classroom, but the assumption is that students will tend to work through the computer-based curriculum independently of what goes on in the classroom. The most stand-alone of these also tend to be the least open-ended in the activities they provide; a human teacher is needed to evaluate free responses, where they occur.

A number of software programs offer practice in a variety of skills, but without extensive management systems or prescriptive curricula. Most expect the learner, often with the help of a teacher, to decide what skills to work on and what media to use. These can range from comprehensive to limited, very expensive to quite affordable. On the high end for English language teaching are programs like Davidson's *English Express* and *Story Club* and American Language Academy's *ALA Lab System*. The Davidson products in particular offer an extensive teachers' manuals to help teachers incorporate the software into their classrooms. In the intermediate price range and with more limited but still extensive content are *MacEnglish* from DynEd and *MacESL* from Hacienda La Puente Adult Education for English language teaching, and The Learning Company's *Learn to Speak* series and Syracuse Language System's *Spanish/French Your Way* for multimedia language instruction in a variety of languages. Most of these products have some sort of record-keeping, though not as extensive as that of the more expensive systems.

Where the computer is not seen as a substitute for a teacher, schools may purchase smaller, more limited, but more flexible software that individual teachers will use as an add-on to instruction or that will be placed in libraries as language references and resources. Language teachers have been especially blessed in this category of software, with hundreds of programs available. The benefits of adding a computer component to language instruction are many, and include

(1) multimodal practice with feedback

(2) individualization in a large class

(3) pair and small group work on projects, either collaboratively or competitively

(4) the fun factor

(5) variety in the resources available and learning styles used

(6) exploratory learning with large amounts of language data

(7) real-life skill-building in computer use

One of the great benefits of the growth of multimedia is that software vendors (and language teachers) no longer feel bound to grammar practice as the main goal of computer use in the language classroom. While the process has taken longer in the foreign language arena than in English language teaching, the movement toward communicative teaching with computers is clearly taking place.

There are still a great many grammar and vocabulary drill programs available, but at least the vocabulary ones have started to be contextualized and to incorporate graphics, audio recording and playback, and video. Drills do have a place in language learning, particularly in the first stages of vocabulary acquisition where giving the same information in multiple modes, such as visual plus aural plus textual, enhances recognition and recall.

More sophisticated error-checking can provide students real help in the feedback they receive, directing them to further practice or moving them to the next stage. Those who do need extra help with those aspects of language that improve with practice can use small, focused programs to give them additional time and assistance outside of regular class time. Pronunciation work in particular has benefited from multimedia. Most pronunciation programs now incorporate some sort of voice recording and playback to let students compare their recording with a model. Many of the English pronunciation programs, such as Ellis Master Pronunciation from CALI, American Accent Program from Ford Language Institute, and American SpeechSounds from Speech Communication, have video clips and animations of the mouth making specific sounds.

Some vocabulary programs, such as Practice Makes Perfect and Vocabulary Builder from The Learning Company, See It, Hear It, Say It! from Courseware Publishing International, and Triple Play Plus from Syracuse Language Systems, use speech recognition technology to help students see how close they've come to the target pronunciation in several languages. A few programs, such as SpeechViewer from IBM and VideoVoice from MicroVideo, let students try to make the graphical representations of their speech overlap a teacher-recorded template. These visual cues work in conjunction with aural cues to provide sophisticated feedback.

Most drills now include games, as well, using the power of the computer and competition for or a collaboration toward a goal—the fun factor—to motivate language learning. Notable among the drill-as-game are Blackbelt Japanese from Educorp; English, French, Spanish, and German versions of Hangman (Hangman, La Guillotine, La Corrida de Toros, and Apfelschuss) from Gessler; Matchmaster from Wida; and Word Attack! from Davidson. These programs provide a varying amount of instruction along with the games, but all expect the teacher to do most of the work in introducing the concepts that students will practice.

Games and the fun factor are not only for drills. A large panel in the tapestry of language learning software is made up of programs designed for collaborative work, where the language that takes place in the pair or small group of students in front of the computer is as if not more important than the language on the computer screen. Early examples of this are Chris Jones's Kingdom and Fast Food, text-based simulations of staying in power and making money on a food booth, respectively. The computer served as the dice-roller, deciding whether natural disasters or scarce supplies would occur to affect the results of the decisions the students had made.

A multimedia version of the same type of program is found in the Carmen Sandiego series from Broderbund and Who Is Oscar Lake? from Gessler, available in a variety of languages. Traci Talk from Courseware Publishing International has added a speech recognition element to the multimedia mystery story it provides, encouraging students to speak to the computer as well as to each other. One of the most sophisticated simulations is A la Rencontre de Philippe from Yale University Press. This interactive video program has the learner help Philippe find an apartment by reading ads, listening to answering machines, looking at maps, and using a wide variety of authentic resources in French. The high quality of the video in this program is in part due to its use of videodisc, so the pictures can be larger and clearer than digitized video would provide. Dunkel and Crookall, et al. describe in detail some of the many advantages of using simulations for language learning.

Collaboration and competition can be built into almost any type of language learning activity, on and off the computer. The classic strip story, where each student adds a sentence to that of the immediately-preceding student without seeing anyone else's sentences, can take an electronic turn with any word-processor that includes the facility for hiding text. Text reconstruction programs such as cloze activities and sentence jumbles or crossword puzzles will become less frustrating and more satisfying when students are collaborating to find the missing words; their partnership against the machine motivates them to keep trying. Even drills are more interesting when students can discuss their answers and try to figure out their mistakes.

Although much of what is done at the computer can be done in other ways, some activities are far more productive with the resources that the computer can bring to bear. Text reconstruction is a good example. A teacher can create a sentence jumble by cutting up pieces of paper, but programs such as NewReader from Hyperbole can do it painlessly. With a paper cloze, students who get stuck on a word have to give up completely and look at the whole text (or ask the teacher individually for a specific answer); on the computer, they can get a letter or word as a hint and go on. Both NewReader from Hyperbole and Text Tanglers from

Research Design Associates can create a variety of text reconstruction activities for a plain-text word-processed document, greatly expanding any classroom reading that the teacher has prepared.

Crossword and word search puzzles are examples of activities that take a great deal of time to prepare by hand, but very little time to do on the computer. The teacher types in a series of words, and the machine formats them appropriately. With a crossword puzzle, the teacher is then prompted for each clue, and the machine formats the whole crossword with clues on the page to be worked on the computer or printed out. Because the process is easy, students can create crosswords for each other. A program like *Crossword Creator* from Centron adds a thesaurus, making it even easier for students and teachers to formulate clues.

The writing process is another area where computers have added a great deal of value. Some programs, such as *IdeaFisher* from IdeaFisher Systems and *Inspiration* from Inspiration Software, help students in the pre-writing stage to generate and outline ideas. Most word-processors now come with spelling checkers, giving weak spellers some help in finding their errors and recognizing the correct spelling from a list of options.

Dictionaries, both translating ones like the Collins On-Line Dictionaries from Harper/Collins and monolingual ones like Softkey's American Heritage Dictionary from Softkey, the Longman Dictionary , and the Oxford English Dictionary for English, and Gessler's Key into French/German/Spanish for those languages, can run in the background and be accessed with a keystroke. Many dictionaries incorporate some grammar help, and some, like the Longman Multimedia Dictionary, have sound and video clips to help learners recognize a word when it's spoken and put it into context. For beginning literacy students, Hartley's My Words and Teacher Support Software's Language Experience Recorder, as well as a number of word-processors, have text-to-speech capability. The quality of text-to-speech software has improved dramatically over time, but the speech is still not particularly natural-sounding. For accurate translation into speech, the computer also generally needs to be running the appropriate language-specific operating system.

Computers are very good at storing, manipulating, and retrieving large amounts of information, making them particularly useful in the area of "data-driven learning." This concept, popularized by Tim Johns, refers to giving students large quantities of language data and the tools to examine it. Students can then build their own explanations of how language works. Having discovered the linguistic rules themselves, students are more likely to remember and use them. Where a teacher may be able to come up on the spur of the moment with a few sentences showing, for example, the use of the past perfect, a concordance program such as Oxford's MicroConcord, Longman's Longman Mini-Concordancer, and Athelstan's Monoconc for Windows could generate hundreds from a large quantity of source text.

Corcordancers, programs that scan large quantities of text for specified words or phrases and present the target words or phrases with a bit of context, have moved gradually from the realm of Biblical and linguistic research into the language classroom. Intermediate and advanced students can use the concordancer themselves to research the usage of a particular word or grammatical structure, while teachers of beginning students can look through the concordancer's results to select appropriate examples for use in class. Domain-specific textbases can be compared to show how usage can change, depending on the setting. Current computers with the processing power to work quickly through thousands of words have made classroom use of concordancers practical.

A related way of examining usage, also using a large textbase, is in finding collocations for words—the words most likely to occur in conjunction with or quite close to a target word. For example, common collocations of the word "charge" would be "in" (in charge) and "take" (take charge), as well as "of" (charge of) and "with" (charge with). Students could also see that "office chair" was a possibility, but not "chair office." Adam and Eve from Oxford University Press finds collocations and helps teachers create different kinds of exercises from a textbase.

A somewhat serendipitous effect of using multimedia, the Internet, and collaborative tasks in language learning is the real-world benefit to students of becoming more sophisticated in using computers and more experienced with a group approach to projects. Computer use is taken for granted in modern companies, and more and more businesses feel the need for an Internet presence, especially as they grow larger. Schools of business in the US now routinely have students work in groups on case studies and other problems to prepare them for the team approach required of executives in many businesses. Collaborative language learning with computers fits right into this real-world model.

Requirements of ICT-based Education Systems

Improving the quality of education is one of the central aims of ICT in schools. Over the last two decades there has been a shift in focus from teacher to learning and a desire the support the development of each individual. Those teachers who have acquired the necessary competencies to work with the Internet increasingly expect to have access to:

— tools for students to develop communication and information processing skills (retrieval engines to find content on the Web, E-mail, chat forums, conferences and news groups in order to communicate with others, tools to allow students to create and present intranet/ Internet content)

— ready-to-use Internet learning materials in electronic form (Web sites offering learning resources which are kept up-to-date)

— content in the form of modular "building blocks" which can be adapted, assembled and used by teachers and their pupils on school intranets

— pedagogical tools for use by teachers to handle the didactics of a given subject area (for example tools from the EC project MALTED for teaching foreign languages, simple tools for analysing and presenting biological data from field studies)

— resources for in-service training and certification of teachers in the use of ICT in education

— tools for supervision and assessment (including examinations)

As the Internet has been in use in mainstream school education for less than five years, there is still a wide gap between education ambitions and the hard reality of daily practice. Whereas surfing the Internet and playing computer and console games are part and parcel of youth culture in many parts of the world, the Net is far from being a natural and integral part of the average teacher's personal and professional development. Figures from New Zealand - a country with progressive attitudes to Internet use in education - bear this out.

— Only about 20% of primary schools reported in 1998 that a quarter or more teaching staff use Internet email during a typical school week. Slightly fewer use the World Wide Web.

— Just over half the schools report that some students would use Internet e-mail at school during a typical week (51% primary, 67% secondary).

— Some student usage of the World Wide Web was slightly more common (62% primary, 76% secondary). Use by a quarter or more of students in a week was relatively rare.

— The 1998 results appear to be a clear increase compared with earlier surveys.

— Buying, maintaining and supporting equipment still accounts for over 75% of school operating funds for the Internet, with less than 15% going to teacher training and content development.

While there is an acceptance of the need to pay for hardware and telecommunications charges, the Internet is still regarded as a kind of electronic "buffet" of content and tools to which anyone can help himself. Although teachers in the past have been used to buying books and audio-visual materials, there is still an expectation that Internet content should be free.

From the point of view of middle-class pupils and parents in the USA and northern Europe, the use of ICT in publicly-funded schools is often regarded as an anachronism. Criticism usually boils down to these arguments:

— there are too few computers in relation to the number of pupils;

— computers in schools are not as up-to-date as computers in homes;

— technical and educational support for ICT in schools is inadequate or non-existent;

— as computers are a scarce resource, they are used in an artificial way in specialised rooms which have to be booked;

— pupils therefore spend far less time on computers at school than they do elsewhere.

Parents in such homes often motivate the purchase of a second computer along with Internet access and some CD-ROMs with the need to give their children a good start in life by supplementing school use of ICT. In Denmark, home spending on education and learning is thought to be between two and four times the amount spent annually on educational materials in the school system. This represents an additional or even an alternative market for educational resources on the Internet.

Vocational and Tertiary Education

On of the terms currently used in discussions about ICT is the Knowledge Society. As the creation of wealth is not just a question of producing material goods but also one of generating knowledge, recent studies indicate knowledge development in societies such as Sweden and German account for more than 10% of GNP. In much of northern Europe, 1 - 2.5% of GNP is spent on vocational education and training in its broadest sense. In vocational education and training and in tertiary education, the main issue is not only that of improving quality. Given the shift in emphasis from pre-service education and training to lifelong learning, adults will need to make use of the education system throughout their working lives to update existing skills and learn new. The agenda also includes improvements to the accessibility and flexibility of educational provisions while at the same time maintaining or even reducing unit costs. In these areas the Internet is a means of providing complete open or distance learning modules and courses to students on or off campus. It also requires specialised tools for collaborative working across networks including desktop audio and video conferencing.

In addition to government funding of Internet content, there are currently 6 dominant business models for content on the Internet:

1. payments from telecommunications companies for generating traffic
2. advertising
3. sponsorship
4. subscriptions
5. pay-per-use
6. cross-media promotion and sales

Payments from Telecommunications Companies

For educational content aimed at schools, the author knows of no instances of telecommunications companies paying for educational content to increase the number of page impressions and user sessions on a host site. This may well be linked to the unacceptability of advertising on school sites. If the traffic by school users only generates revenue in the form of connection charges and does not also lead to e-commerce elsewhere on the site, the financial incentive of the telecommunications company is somewhat limited.

In the first few years of Internet use in schools, telecommunications companies such as TELIA in Sweden funded the development of educational content on the Web. Individual teachers and schools were expected to find the guidelines on the TELIA site, submit their proposal electronically and then work in close collaboration with TELIA who then helped maintain the web site with the materials produced. This activity may well have been paid for by the research and development/marketing department as a kind of sponsorship.

TELECOM NEW ZEALAND was also one of the earliest to support the provision of learning kits on the net. They covered topics such as vulcanism and the ozone layer over the poles and included opportunities for schools to communicate with scientists in the Antarctic about their work. In theory, advertising could be used as a business model for supporting some kinds of Internet-based learning activity in the home.

Sponsorship

DR is a public service broadcaster in Denmark operating with revenues from a licence fee. Since 1996 DR Multimedia have been working on cross-media projects consisting of television, radio and the Web for the education system. The objective from DR's side has been to assure financially self-sustaining production of resources which can support and enrich educational provisions in Denmark. As DR's production of Internet materials could not until recently be funded by revenue from the broadcasting licence, an interim business model was found to cover the setting up of Web projects of limited duration.

The first two projects of this kind were "Africa in the Backwaters" for geography, English and French as a foreign language, and "Climate on the Web" for environmental education. Perhaps the most visible example of sponsorship is the UK supermarket chain Tesco which sponsors a massive site called Schoolnet 2000. The site acts as a point of contact for 15,000 schools and to date almost 60,000 pupils have produced materials which have been uploaded into one of the many thematic areas on the site.

The sponsorship model requires an analysis of the market to identify interested parties willing to sponsor the project. In the case of the Africa project, some of the funding came from the Ministry of Education fund for educational resource development and was augmented by contributions from the Ministry of Foreign Affairs. For the "Climate on the Net" project, funding was forthcoming the Ministry for the Environment and from the Danish Environmental Board. The sponsors were credited on the web site and the funds were taken from their information budgets.

The sponsorship model lends itself to the development of professional, ready-to-use Internet learning resources which would not otherwise be produced by teachers and students themselves. Its weakness is that only certain curriculum areas are suitable. It is highly unlikely that controversial subjects would be supported, in much the same way that sponsorship in the Arts tends to concentrate on well-established art forms at the expense of more experimental works.

Subscriptions

Before the emergence of on-line services on the Internet, on-line database services used in schools and colleges were funded by subscriptions. Of particular interest here are databases from daily newspapers and at vocational and tertiary level, professional databases such as DIALOG which include ERIC.

In Europe, some of these educational subscriptions to on-line databases have succeeded in making the transition to Internet delivery; some new instances of subscription models for learning materials have recently appeared such as the Danish Electronic Marketplace for Education (EMU) run for the Danish Ministry of Education by UNI-C. This is a virtual marketplace for educational content in digital form which can be used to deliver content or to provide information on other educational resources such as multimedia CD-ROMs and audio-visual materials. Publishers and developers pay the equivalent of "rent" for their virtual shop and they also pay a handling charge for content to cover the handling of payments and IPR issues for digital content accessed and used by schools.

In general it is still premature to assess whether this business model will take root in schools, whereas it is already a success elsewhere. A number of vocational and tertiary modules and courses are available over the Internet for lifelong learning. Where they are part of distance education and open learning provisions they can be paid for either directly - a kind of subscription - or indirectly in the form of fees for the final examination or for face-to-face sessions. There is an increasing number of private courses being offered in this way either directly with conditional access via the Internet or delivered and installed on in-house intranets for use by companies.

Pay-per-use

With the emergence of secure mechanisms for handling payments e-commerce via the Internet and a variety of schemes for digital cash for micro-payments, this business model would seem to have considerable potential. The drawbacks for school users centre on the practicalities of administering such schemes. Who decides what resources are to be used, and who is responsible if pupils make unauthorised purchases? At vocational and tertiary level, in particular when it comes to using tools and services, there does seem to be considerable scope in particular for students on distance education courses. An example of this was an experimental service operated by BT (the British telecommunications company) for producing automated summaries using a tool called ProSumm. Users could either buy the tool as a Microsoft Word plug-in or pay a few cents per Internet page with a micro-payments scheme.

Cross-media Promotion and Sales

Given that the Internet is still commonly regarded as a source of free content by teachers and parents alike, revenues to pay for the development, delivery and maintenance of Internet content can come from other media within a cross-media educational package. Revenue educational resources on the Internet may in fact come from enrolment or matriculation fees for distance education.

Public service broadcasters such as the BBC use the Internet to promote the core activities and have been allowed to produce Web and digital television content for education as part of their public service obligations. Publishers may well use the Web to promote the sale of textbooks and multimedia on CD-ROM and DVD.

Educational resources on the Internet are thus appetisers to promote the sales of other media. In the school, commercial publishers may choose to sell learning kits including student books, teaching guides, a CD-ROM and a video where the sale of these components generates revenue for Internet materials. An instance of this is an environmental education project with the title "Death in Slow Motion" currently being developed by DR, the Danish publisher Malling Beck, and partners in Europe and elsewhere. The hybrid CDROM in this package is to provide access to an educational Intranet where pupils can access updated information and exchange their work with pupils at other schools both nationally and internationally.

In the home, cross-media projects involving the Internet paradoxically may lead to a renewed interest in CDROMs. Cross-media projects combined with some kind of electronic payment may well be one of the most interesting business models for educational publishers entering this field. In a session on the Internet, Ann Foster of Reed Educational & Professional quoted UK figures for the revenue generated by publishing textbooks and on-line educational resources indicating that on-line still accounted for less than 1% of total spending. Ann Foster reiterated that there is currently not a lot of money to be earned by commercial companies in the school system. From a commercial point of view, technology-supported learning in the home is considerably more viable.

Bibliography

Frost, L.A., & Bondy, A.S., *The picture exchange communication system: Training manual*, Cherry Hill, NJ: Pyramid Educational Consultants, Inc, 1994

Gantt, V. W., "The Case Method in Teaching Critical Thinking", *Paper presented at the Annual Meeting of the Southern States Communication Association* (Memphis, TN, March 27-31). ERIC Accession No. ED399597, 31 March 1996.

Gardner, P. S., "Makers and Users of Knowledge: Literary Re-Creation in the Classroom", *Journal of Teaching Writing*, 11(1) 19-33.

Garrett, M., Schoener, L., & Hood, L., "Debate: A teaching strategy to improve verbal communication and critical-thinking skills", *Nurse Educator*, 21(4), 37-40.

Geske, J., "Overcoming the drawbacks of the large lecture class", *College Teaching*, 40 (4) 151-154.

Giordano, P.J. & Hammer, E.Y., "In-class collaborative learning: Practical suggestions from the teaching trenches", *Teaching of Psychology*, 26(1), 42-44.

Gleason-Weimer, M., "Better communication in large courses", *College Teaching*, 34(1), 20-24.

Gordon, H. G., "Using a Reading Response Journal", *Teaching English in the Two-Year College*, 28(1), 41-43, 2000.

Haddad, A.M., "Teaching ethics as a writing-intensive, ability-based course", *Journal of Pharmacy Teaching*, 6(1/2), 49-64, 1997.

Hoban, G., "Using a reflective framework for experiential education in teacher education classes", *Journal of Experiential Education*, 22(2), 104-111, Fall,1999

Hodgdon, L.A., *Visual strategies for improving communication: Practical supports for school and home* (Vol. 1). Troy, MI: QuirkRoberts Publishing, 1995.

Quill, K.A., *Teaching children with autism: Strategies to enhance communication and socialization*, New York, NY: Delmar Publishers, Inc., 1995.

Quill, K.A., *D0-watch-listen-say: Social and communication intervention for children with autism*, Baltimore, MD: Paul H. Brookes Publishing. ISBN: 1-55766-453-6, 2000

Index